P9-DVG-128

Books by William Gibson

THE SEESAW LOG, *with the text of* TWO FOR THE SEESAW
(1959)

THE MIRACLE WORKER
(1957)

THE COBWEB
(1954)

These are BORZOI BOOKS
published by Alfred A. Knopf in New York

THE SEESAW LOG

with the text of

TWO *for the* SEESAW

THE SEESAW LOG

a chronicle of the stage production,

with the text, of TWO *for the* SEESAW

by William Gibson

ALFRED A. KNOPF *New York* 1959

L. C. Catalog card number: 59–6218

THIS IS A BORZOI BOOK,
PUBLISHED BY ALFRED A. KNOPF, INC.

 Manufactured in the United States of America. Published simultaneously in Canada by McClelland & Stewart Ltd.

FIRST EDITION

for Massie and the boys

WHOSE EXISTENCE BEFORE, DURING, AND AFTER

MAKES FAILURE AND SUCCESS

A STUFF OF DREAMS

Contents

THE SEESAW LOG 1

TWO FOR THE SEESAW 143

THE SEESAW LOG

WILLIAM GIBSON

ACT ONE

Spring 1953 – *Fall* 1957

This narrative is a minute piece of contemporary history, a log of the adventures or misadventures of a playscript, not to mention a virginal playwright, en route to Broadway.

I began writing it midway in the play's career, when the script was finished and the production first contracted for; I set myself to record its life and hard times as they occurred. But I noted that I had been at this point before. The script was my sixth, and I knew the theater was a world in which betwixt the cup and the lip there was a long avenue of abandoned vehicles, five of them mine; if the log reached print it would be only because the production had actually taken place, and been either a success or a failure. I thus commenced the log in ignorance of what its contents would be, if indeed any.

For me, it was to serve two purposes: it would provide me with a balloon above the battlefield, into which I could climb to lick my wounds; and in the event of total carnage, I would salvage a written account of it—not a negligible yield for any writer to whom language rather than theatrical performance is the solid coin of the realm. For others, I thought the log might serve to document the theater conditions under which a play was produced in mid-century; such a log from a generation ago, of any play, would sidelight some of our most eminent stage literature. I knew it would be, whatever its accidents of personnel or event, a characteristic record. Even for me its interest lies not in its singularity: any of the participants in our production, or in any other production, could such a tale unfold, different in viewpoint or facts, but equally harassed by the complexities of group action; and the portrait of contemporary theater in each would be in this essence identical.

The opening section was written at scattered times prior to the onset of rehearsals. Thereafter, though I hopefully carried the log with me, I had no leisure to add a word to it; instead, I kept a notebook in which I scribbled the gist and memorable dialogue of each day. The log was completed from these notes, and sent to each of the principals, for corrections and deletions, prior to publication.

It is less than the truth, in several ways. First, I have censored much that was overpersonal; only in fiction can one tell the truth. Secondly, it is in language, and language alters events; the events were everyone's, the language is mine, and refracts solely my view of something less than the truth; and my view was that of a man who at no point took for granted the premises of show business. And thirdly, it is exaggerated in humor; needless to add, the sensitive reader—I add it for other kinds—will understand that exaggeration is used herein to tone the truth down. The truth was much worse.

2

FIRST, the play was written.

The image for it came to me one sleepless night in a lumpy bed on a visit to New York; such are the rewards of the literary mind. This was early in 1953. I was then in the middle of writing a novel, *The Cobweb*, which I did not finish until fall, and so it was November before I first sat down to write the play. All I managed was a title and part of the first scene. I was floundering among several pieces I wanted to write, or thought I thought I did, and other pieces I did not want to write but was committed to, such as a pageant script to celebrate the centennial of Omaha, a city I had never set foot in; I was still to direct two plays for an amateur drama group in a psychiatric institution where I was employed, and one of these was an earlier script of my own which I did a new version of, early in 1954; and life made other demands on me, I was a new father, which is to say a new man whose acquaintance I was making every day, mostly in the early hours, and the novel was published and made a stir, which made another stir in me, and made another in a real-estate agent until he knocked on our door, and I was presently devoting my life to his work, hunting for a house and land he could sell us, and in the summer I went out for the Omaha pageant, and in the fall I went out to Hollywood to do some last-minute patchwork on a movie script of *The Cobweb* that MGM had paid someone $40,000 to write and then would not film. So, what with this and that, I did not get much beyond the first scene of the play that year.

We came home to Massachusetts at the turn of the year with me still astonished at the minimal demands most actors made upon themselves, and somewhat overfed on glamour, like a diet of cream-puff shells; I was resolved not to write a play but another novel. We moved into our own house that spring, which ate up some more time, after which I took over a cottage that came with it and was to be my workplace, sat down in it, and floundered further. I began three or four things, abandoning them as they successively died on me, came back to each in turn, looking in vain for signs of life, tried to begin the play anew as a novel, found it declined to do anything but talk dialogue, and by early summer of 1955 had something that bore a resemblance to a first act.

A friend named Arthur Penn, a quiet, concentrated, and subtly intelligent man in his early thirties who was directing TV plays, drove up for a weekend with his fiancée, a young actress, and I read the act to them; they were so enthusiastic that from then on I flogged only the play, ignoring the other corpses. Two or three times, when I felt unhappy with the rigors of the form, or worried about gambling on the theater, I tried again to begin it as a novel, but it insisted on coming into the world as dialogue. My conscience kept nagging me that writing dialogue was not real work, it left too much still to be done by other hands. As scenes were written, I would read them to my wife, to Arthur and his bride, and to another couple—the director who had succeeded me in the drama group at the institution, and his wife—whose liking for the script perked me up when I sagged. There were two characters in the play, and I was hung up most of the summer over whether to bring in a third or not, trying it both ways, meanwhile polishing the first act so much I wore holes in the paper of two or three retypings of it; but by fall I had escaped out of the first act into the second, and from then through the spring of 1956 it was in a state of movement, often backwards, but alive. I should say half-alive: the girl in the play had pre-empted it from the moment she opened her mouth, and having put most of my internal life into her, I had little left for the man, who remained shadowy. I made a last gesture in the direction of a one-man undertaking when I sent four scenes to my publisher and asked whether they could give me an advance on this as material for a proposed book; they said no, that while it "might make a tight little play" it was "too sparse" for a novel. I disagreed, but this door at least was now shut. Sometime during the winter I saw a particularly good TV show of Arthur's, and when he drove up for a visit the following day I asked him whether he would like to direct the play, when finished and if produced. He said he would be delighted. By the end of April I had a complete draft.

I then collected a dozen friends in New York and read it aloud to them. Among those present were a lawyer who had been counselling me on some legal background used in the script, my agent Leah Salisbury, and my wife. After I finished, everyone criticized the play—essentially, the man in it—for an hour or two, the group disbanded, and I went to bed gloomy. The evening had been neither a disaster nor a success, reaction as a whole had been respectful and unenthusiastic, and I had not learned whether Leah thought she could sell the script.

We came home to the country, I had a half-dozen copies typed, wrote Leah I would not send her any for circulation until I had done another draft, but did mail copies to two men in Hollywood: one was a playwright of genius, a friend since the time I had attended a class of his at the Actors Studio a few years before; the other was Richard Widmark, who had been in the movie of *The Cobweb* and whom I hoped to lure back to the stage in the play, my first act of attempted casting. I gave a second reading, this one in my home, to eight more friends and my wife, a group which responded more gratifyingly, though the same criticisms of my hero's vagueness were made as after the first reading. Arthur drove up as soon as he was done with some out-of-town repairs on a play someone else had been directing, but which folded anyway as soon as it opened in New York, and he and his wife wept over my script; each tear rang reassuringly like money in the bank. We discussed revisions and deletions for the new draft, and by this time, having with my wife's help digested and made some sense out of a confusion of criticisms, I was ready to rewrite the man.

At this point a dismayed letter came from the playwright,

written on a typewriter equipped solely with capital letters and interlineated with vigorous handscript in red ink, saying my play was "poor," "not really a play," "uninteresting," and not salvageable by any counsel he could give; his only advice was to "abandon it, and begin something new." (Arthur said, "He's wrong.") After several days, when my ribs felt unbroken again, I wrote back I did not think the play could be that bad, I couldn't abandon it, his letter would fortify me to expect the worst, but I would proceed with the rewriting I had in mind. I did. In the middle a sweet letter came from Widmark, in a boyishly open handscript, saying he thought the play "skillfully done" and "very good," but he doubted my two characters could hold an audience, he could not "get enthusiastic about their problem," and wished me all luck. I completed the rewriting, and had twenty-five copies made under the title *Two for the Seesaw*. I mailed five to Leah, and I gave another five to Arthur, who had driven up again to talk over a TV script which in my worry about money I had proposed I do for him. It was the end of June, 1956.

I arranged a third reading, to try out the new draft. This one again took place in my house, to a group of six friends and my wife, who by this time was eligible for any medal given for valor under erosion. The reaction was as unexcited as at the first reading, and the criticisms of the man were identical, despite the weeks I had put into rewriting him.

Five days later our second boy was born, needing a new pair of shoes.

Letters now came in from friends in Connecticut, Kansas, California, to whom I had sent copies: one found it "intensely absorbing" and "could not put it down," another "didn't know whether he thought it interesting or not," another was "delighted with it," another thought it "drab," another said it was "not a play" and—new note—should be turned into a novel. Leah wrote me it was "moving, funny, strange, and greatly improved in the rewriting," and that she would "do her best"; I still had no idea whether she thought it saleable. All I knew was that I had a script which some individuals liked very much, some did not like at all, and some, probably most, liked only somewhat.

By now I felt I had done all I could to the material, and was resolved not to touch it again until a producer took an option on it. It had been three years since its conception; for a full year I had been sitting to it eight or ten hours a day, and this thumbnail account of its writing conveys little of the sense of interminable struggle, the worry, the elation, the despondency, the bursts of energy and stretches of impasse, which made up that year. These were birth pangs I was used to and happy with. But in any literary form I would now be at their end; what dismayed me about the stage was the prospect of delivering the same baby over and over again, with a high likelihood of stillbirth. Meanwhile, I had turned ten copies loose for marketing in the big city, there was nothing more I could do.

I began work on something else, and waited.

3

The rejections began to come in.

Arthur had spoken about the play to his own agent, who had spoken to two producers, with the result that I received a letter from number one and my agent received a phone call from number two, both asking to see the script. Leah sent copies to them. Number one then took off to London, and the first rejection came from number two, very promptly. Leah wrote me that he found the play interesting but it did not "excite" him and he thought "these two characters couldn't hold an audience." We waited for number one, who went to Moscow. Leah sent a copy to number three; this producer wrote that she was "most enthusiastic" about my talents and "predicted a great future" for me, not knowing I already had one foot in the grave, but suspected the play "did not have enough meat to sustain over an entire evening with just the two characters." A friend delivered a copy to a representive of a producing organization, number four, whose opinion was that it was not typed correctly. Number five told Arthur he would be interested in the script only if it were changed this way and that in the direction of commercial comedy; the changes were so ruinous to my point that Arthur did not even acquaint me with them. We waited for number one, who went to the Democratic convention in Chicago.

Arthur earlier had given a copy to Fred Coe, a TV producer of considerable influence for whom Arthur had directed several dozen shows and who had produced one stage play in collaboration with the Theatre Guild, not a commercial success. Arthur phoned me one night in August with two pieces of news. The first was that number one was back in New York, had read the play, thought it very skillfully written, had reservations about its dramatic effectiveness in the character of the man, already had three scripts to produce that season, and preferred to work on Stevenson's presidential campaign. The second was that Fred Coe thought the play was the best script he had seen in a long time, would like to produce it, and was contacting my agent.

I bought a new suit, the first summer-weight suit I ever owned, and drove down to the city to meet Coe in Leah's office. He was a younger man than I expected, in I judged his late thirties, quietly dressed, unhurried, reserved behind his eyeglasses; he made no effort to impress me favorably, and that impressed me favorably. We felt out each other's taste and temperament, which was essentially the object of the meeting. Leah pressed for two points, a production in the season immediately at hand and a cast of two stars; Coe was pleasant and unargumentative, but committed himself to neither. We spoke then chiefly of casting, as the paramount problem in a two-character play, and Leah and he exchanged a host of suggestions, ranging from probably unobtainable—and by me unwanted—stars to players I had never heard of. Leah suggested among others Henry Fonda, but Coe thought him not in the age range of the man as written and I thought him too straightforward. One name agreeable to all was Gwen Verdon, and Coe moved promptly: before we left the office he had learned by phone what her present and future commitments were, and within three hours he, Arthur, and I had scrutinized her in a matinee, talked with her backstage, and left a script with her. I drove home convinced that Coe would be an effective man to work with, and what doubts I had come with, concerning the brevity of his experience as a stage producer, were largely gone.

I conveyed my feeling to Leah, who shared it, and negotiations to sell Coe the play were begun. I should explain that a producer "buys" a play by taking an option on it for an agreed-upon period, during which he has sole right to produce it; the option money he pays to the playwright is given as an advance on royalties, and if the play is not produced within the period specified, all rights revert to the author, who keeps the advance. There is no ceiling to this advance, but minimal terms of $200 a month are fixed by the Dramatists Guild, to which all playwrights belong and which therefore operates in the theater as a closed-shop union. Leah said she would ask for an advance of $1,000, and I told her I preferred $2,500. After that I heard nothing further for two or three weeks, and I fretted.

Arthur and I spoke on the phone one night in September about the TV script we were doing together, and he said he felt that negotiations on *Two for the Seesaw* had bogged down; he surmised Leah's position to be that if Coe could get two stars she would let him have the play and Coe's position to be that we were uneager to have him. I thereupon phoned Leah in the city, found her not at home, and phoned Coe at his summer place on Long Island. We greeted each other by first names—the instant quasi-intimacy which is de rigueur in the theater, for reasons I am willing to leave to social psychologists to educe—and he said the difficulty was mainly one of time: Leah was offering him only an eight-months option, to comprise the present season, and he felt he needed twelve, to go into the season following if need be. But also he thought Leah's casting suggestions, though of undoubted stars, were not always compatible with his view of the play. I replied that while I always listened to Leah's opinions, they were not necessarily mine. We set a date to meet with Arthur, to see whether our views were congenial; he thanked me for calling, said it gave him "more confidence," and when we hung up, I called Leah again. It was almost midnight before I reached her. She told me her reason for not offering a longer period was that she wanted to be free next summer to sell the script to someone else for the season following if Coe failed to produce it; if he held it until fall, and then failed, we would lose the next season as well. I said I would like him to have the twelve months he wanted, and after more talk she yielded, without enthusiasm. She thought I was mistaken to think she had communicated any feeling of uneagerness, stated flatly, "I want that man," and said she would call him again in the morning.

It was mid-September when Arthur and I met with Fred in his office, a large airy room on the twenty-eighth floor in Radio City. We talked exclusively casting. During this discussion it became evident enough that if our tastes differed none of us would be inaccessible to reason, and when I left the meeting it was with word that Fred's agent would call mine the following day. Negotiations were back on the tracks.

They remained on the tracks, motionless, for another two months. Letters and phone calls went between me and Arthur, me and Leah, but I never learned what really caused the delay, other than the hardships of agents and lawyers in calling each other back. During these weeks I often thought I would never see the contract in hand, and I kept fretting; but one noon in mid-November, while a friend and I were hammering at a one-room studio we were putting up for me on our hilltop, four fat copies of twenty-nine pages each arrived for my signature, already bearing Fred's, and a very attractive signature it was. The term was six months with an advance of $1,500, renewable for another six at $1,500 more, beginning October 3, 1956. I read, signed, and mailed the contracts back within the hour, and hammered for another week while the Dramatists Guild pored over them. The last difficulty was removed when Fred's lawyer, at the Guild's enjoining, deleted a phrase in which I promised "not to unreasonably withhold approval" of the cast and director in any British production, which at this point seemed as imminent to me as one on Mars. The Guild then countersigned, and accepted Fred's check. When my payment finally drifted in it was minus my agent's 10% and the Guild's 2% assessment, and came to $1,320, the first money I had earned in two years.

It was not quite five months since the play had gone to market. I had a producer.

4

WE WERE in business, but on such a shaky scaffolding that I was counting on little beyond the option money. We had a script whose general appeal was so far from certain I felt there was an element of fraud in selling it to anyone; what was certain was that any serious error in casting or staging would result in our producing a two-character catastrophe. We had a forty-two-year-old author who over twenty years of trying had never had a play produced in the professional theater; I had a good bit of experience as an actor and director in amateur theater, had watched top professionals make an uninteresting movie from a not uninteresting novel, and thought (with some private tremors) I preferred to trust my own judgments in the theater thereafter; and I had opened the door for these by choosing a director myself—but a friend who

I was assured liked my work, and about whose work in turn I knew I could not be objective. We had thus a young director whose experience was almost totally in TV; he had done one stage play as a summer tryout, and redone another in its final week on the road; and he had taken my script to a TV producer to whom his own work was much more familiar and successful than it was in the theater. We had thus a producer of the first rank in his own world, but with only one stage play behind him, and whose most recent TV series had lost its sponsor; currently he was inactive; I felt in part he was groping, and his hand happened on my script. And we had my agent, a woman of fierce loyalty—one of the few people in the world whose personal allegiance I completely trusted—who had been representing me for twenty years, during most of which her earnings from my collected works would not have bought her shoelaces; she had a long list of successful plays to her name, and I doubted that she thought mine likely to be added to it; certainly I knew she was worried at my bringing it to her with a green director already attached, and I took her insistence on the need for stars to be an expression of all her misgivings.

Now, out of this four-way circling of semi-doubts and semi-convictions, we began upon the production.

5

WHEREUPON almost a year passed. Much half-happened in the course of this year, but until its final quarter nothing conclusive enough to warrant carrying my log further; and at one point it seemed it was destined only for the fireplace. What beset us during most of this period was solely the problem of casting.

This problem had two centers, at best difficult to make coincide: fidelity to what I had written, and commercial feasibility. Ideally, we were after two stars, texturally suitable to the parts, and technically resourceful enough to hold the stage without reinforcements for two hours, whose names would assure us of an audience; that prospect would in turn assure us not only of financing for the production, but of a theater to play in. This was hardly a negligible item, since theaters are scarce, projects are plentiful and competitive, theater owners share heavily in the profits of a show, and without the likelihood of sizeable profits a theater is simply not rentable. But the difficulty in casting the girl was that she was very specifically written, a Jewish gamin from the Bronx, and not one of the eminent actresses we named had anything of her quality. Conversely, the man was so unspecifically written that one actor's name sounded as appropriate as another's, which bemused us all. In both instances we were inviting an actor to expose his talents, if any, in a naked light for an entire evening. Younger actors, who had nothing to lose but obscurity, would jump at this opportunity; to established stars we expected it would seem a more perilous boon, and indeed it did.

I will not tabulate the score of names we discussed and vetoed—any that come to the reader's mind came as readily to ours—but only the score we acted upon. These fell into categories of prestige: with some, simple submission of the script was tantamount to an unretractable offer of the part; with others, less celebrated, submission was only exploratory, but their status forbade our inviting them in to "read" for us; still others would read repeatedly, within reason.

We had begun with the girl by giving Gwen Verdon a script; she somewhat gradually declined. Fred phoned for my permission to offer it to Julie Harris, who I said was not in fact or fiction a Jewish girl from the Bronx, but for box-office reasons I assented, and felt the worm of corruption stir; Miss Harris redeemed me by being unable to "see herself" in it. With like thoughts we sent a copy to Kim Stanley, who redeemed me by never replying. Fred submitted it to another star, and the word came back that she "loved" it, our first affirmative response from an actress of note, which cheered us all, but I had never seen her work. We spoke of entraining the following week for Chicago, where she was playing, and pending this Fred arranged for me to view her in a TV kinescope; I thought her too remote from my Bronx girl, and the Chicago jaunt evaporated.

What passes in a paragraph here in actual passage took weeks. During these weeks we were also investigating other actresses, whom we could request to read for us. I drove to New York in November and December to listen to Lee Grant, Barbara Baxley, and Gaby Rodgers read pieces of the play with Arthur in Fred's office in Radio City, where the shadow of my agent's disapproval fell upon us from 44th Street; she said to me over the phone, "I thought you were going after stars." These office readings indeed seemed scant evidence on which to base a choice that might cost the lot of us literally a million dollars. While Arthur and Fred appeared untroubled by it, I was frightened and indecisive. I asked for repeat readings, pursued Miss Grant on records and in a TV kinescope of a show I had already seen, and arose from a sickbed to drive from Stockbridge to New Haven for a look with Fred at Miss Rodgers onstage. This was early in January 1957; Arthur had flown to Hollywood, where he was to work for the next nine months, and I felt as though a foot were missing. But that month I came through the fog of issues to a solid perception: every choice entailed the risk of mistake and failure, and the most demoralizing mistake to live with would be one made purely in terms of box office. I wrote Arthur, Fred, and Leah that despite my terrors the actress I thought closest to my girl, and whom I therefore wanted, was Lee Grant. Arthur wrote back he wanted her too, Fred was noncommittal, and Leah in her vexation at my ignoring of economic realities told me I didn't have "a grain of theater sense." The moral solidity of the perception rattled.

Simultaneously we had been approaching men, uncertain what we wanted, only certain the man was second fiddle to the girl and would appear so to every actor who opened the script. Jack Lemmon said no, though it was not clear whether he had opened it first. Paul Newman said possibly, but he was strangling in movie obligations and could not articulate further. In December we had dazzling news: Richard Basehart thought it "the best play he had read in years." We conferred hastily, and moved to grab him. Arthur had lunch with him before his own departure west, Fred opened negotiations with Basehart's agent, and in late January, while in New York en route to Hollywood myself, I had dinner with Basehart, his agent, and a very seductive Fred. For my taste the atmosphere was one of too much courtship, too much connoisseuring of the menu and wine list, and too much speculation about script changes—always a subject to dismay my heart—in the direction of not parting my lovers; I was not overjoyed with any of us. Among the immemorabilia of the conversation was Basehart's suggestion of an actress utterly unknown to me, Anne Bancroft. It was his second mention of her to Fred, who now made a note of it, saying he would see her; I took this as only another curtsy at Basehart, and left to catch a glimpse of a show starring Kim Stanley. She still did not look Jewish to me, and I went to California.

What took me there was the production of *The Miracle Worker*, the TV play I had written for Arthur. I sat in on rehearsals for two weeks, my first view of Arthur at work, and a reassuring one, albeit of an insane world; his hand on all its materials, human and technological, was talented, alert, unfumbling; but my literary conscience stirred uneasily throughout at my relying upon any medium other than language, it was not "serious" in some way that eluded me. We went staggering on the air February 7, with a hit. Twenty minutes after the show I was out of the CBS studio with my suitcase, headed for the airport, home and family, and Miss Bancroft.

That morning Fred had phoned from New York to ask whether I could meet her—"the best Gittel yet"—in his office the next noon, before my train to Massachusetts and her plane to Hollywood. I was sitting there, very skeptical, when she blew in. She was a dark, quick, not pretty but vitally attractive girl with a sidewalk voice that greeted me instantly with, "How was the coast, lousy, huh?" and my mind blinked; she could have walked off my pages. Fred called in an actor for her to read with, and she read excitingly, with the exact turns of voice—this was eerie—I had heard when writing the lines and had not heard since; I felt we had fallen into a diamond-in-the-rough mine. But telling a story minutes later she slid into an elegant characterization, and I perceived she was not a type, but a talent. The minute she left I told Fred I was sold, and we agreed it turned only on what impression she made on Arthur when she reached the coast. She made an impression: he hired her for his next TV show and sent us his opinion, she was "Gittel on the hoof."

All now seemed set, and with a minimum of compromise. We had a good actor in Basehart, and a name that would help us get the money and the theater; we had the one actress in captivity who had been born—a mile from me in the Bronx, and surely Jewish, though she turned out Italian—to play this girl; and she was one Basehart wanted to work with. True, there were shadows in heaven. Miss Bancroft—Annie henceforth to us—had never been on a New York stage; we were gambling on a minor TV and movie actress, whose work in those media I now went out of my way to see and was disappointed by; she might well go up in smoke in a theater. Also, her name pulled no commercial weight on its own. And Basehart was elusive, his agent set high terms, there were mutterings about prohibitive income taxes, and presently he went off to Hollywood, still unsigned. This seemed only a postponement; Fred went to Hollywood himself in March, to film a western with Arthur and Paul Newman, and hoped to sign Basehart and Annie there. Silence descended, while I envisioned everyone cavorting after Basehart along the Pacific. It was weeks before I heard we had definitely lost him.

This left us without a name, and with an actress we were all in love with, could not bear to give up, and could not risk signing alone; she was still a diamond in our eyes, but something of a millstone around our necks. Fred and Arthur in the intervals of movie-making looked around on the coast, while I came to a slow simmer in the Berkshire hills, waiting for action. One night they called me with what seemed in some degree a watered-stock list of names, male and female, which under my eye boiled away to nothing. After Annie, the women included two well-known nuts we had earlier declined even to consider, a singing dancer who was charming but not an actress to my taste, a model who had been in a movie where no one said a word, a star I had already vetoed, and Lee Grant; the men comprised seven time-honored favorites, four youthful unfavorites, three TV workhorses, and the most attractive name on the list, Henry Fonda. With Fonda we had come full circle back to the moment of my first meeting with Fred in Leah's office, eight months earlier.

Following this call I began to think, with or without justice, that the production was in jeopardy; I saw standards unravelling, time ditto, the summer was almost upon us, and what loomed on my horizon was a thrown-together show. I turned to Leah for support and the counsel of experience. She came through with much of both, and urged me to let her go after still another celebrated star, in my opinion one of the world's dullest actors. For twenty-four disoriented hours I acceded. It was my wife who brought me up sharp; we talked it over, and I saw that in this instance it was not true the show must go on, I could specify under what conditions I preferred no production at all. This I did in letters to Leah and Fred listing the actors I would accept and those I would not. I said I would go with two stars already in process of receiving scripts, Fonda—which delighted Leah, she went into action to get a second script herself to him in Europe—and Van Heflin, but with no one else in that age range; my real interest was in a younger man, and most particularly one I thought had exceptional talent, Fritz Weaver. This vigorous suggestion was greeted by a vigorous silence.

In the period following, Fred and Arthur relayed word from many other actors, on and off my list. Van Heflin and Paul Newman said maybe, at some length; Jack Palance almost said yes, but said no instead; Jack Lemmon again said no; Barry Nelson, Eli Wallach, Don Murray, and Robert Preston said no. In May I was in New York seeing an opera I had secretly written the libretto for, and in the lobby ran into John Houseman, the director of the American Shakespeare Festival, where Weaver had been a member of the company; Houseman, one of the brightest men I knew, told me Weaver was "a fantastic actor, not for everything, but for intellectual romantic parts the best actor in America." At dawn the next day—dawn in New York is eleven o'clock—I looked Weaver up in the phone book and called him, to learn he had that week signed for another play. It was bitter solace that a week later, having read mine, he told me he thought it "incredibly good."

We had now lost three actors in recent weeks to shows in the coming season, and Weaver had been my private ace in the hole. I took off on a paranoid flight of wrath, a small foible of mine which prolonged dependence on others usually elicited. Time's winged chariot was hurrying up our rear end, and Leah's fears of the twelve-month option had proved justified: after the fall I would myself be unavailable, by reason of a movie job which would kill the balance of the theater season; we had no man, no money, no theater, no designer, no contract with either Annie or Arthur, and no one in the east to mind the store; though we had said several times we were willing to produce without stars, this approach demanded two moves—reserving a theater much earlier, and together exhaustively interviewing New York actors—that time had now passed by; and my producer and director were closeted in Hollywood with cowboys and horses, none of them castable in my play. It was a situation I had no power to act upon, inaction was turning my blood black, and I saw only one way to retain my sanity.

I wrote Arthur I could give no further time or thought to the production, I felt it was a cause lost by forfeit, I was sick to death of the fifty-handed jugglery of show business, and I would henceforth be incommunicado in my studio. This letter cleared what was left of my mind, and one hour later I was at work. I set myself the chore I had failed at before; I typed a remembered sentence from Emerson, "Nothing will bring you peace but the triumph of principle," planted it under the glass on my desk top where it could keep an eye on me, sharpened my crockful of pencils, and sat down to do the play over again, from the beginning, as a novel. And instantly, painlessly, at long last, it sprang to life as narrative. I holed up with it all week, it kept coming, I felt benign as a lark turned loose, at last my own man again in a medium where no one's help stood between me and the audience, and I sent Fred a rational note apologizing for the irritability of my recent letters. In two blissful weeks I wrote twenty pages of the novel; nothing now could stop me.

It was on this rise that news of Fonda broke around my head.

Leah called from New York, and Fred from Hollywood, to apprise me that Fonda was back from Europe, liked the play, and was interested in talking with us; I was the only one within shouting distance. It was now mid-June, 1957. I dressed up in my summer suit once again, same suit, different summer, and drove to the big city. We met in Fonda's home in the east seventies—Fonda, Fred's agent, and I—and discussed all the hotels of Europe, where I had never been, and the script. Fonda could not say yes outright, it seemed to be hurting him not to, what prevented him was his feeling that the man was underwritten; it was a view I could not think wrongheaded, though I longed to. His manner, while not inviting of easy contact, was decent and modest, he had no other reservations or demands such as any star might well make—choice of actress or director, for example—and I drove back to Massachusetts with the problem like a sack of coal in my lap. I had been boiling for weeks that I was impotent to affect our luck, and the devil had answered my prayers: if we got Fonda all other difficulties would vanish, and getting him now depended on no one but me. It meant dropping the novel, it meant drowning again in the collaborative gluepot of the theater, and worst of all, it meant rewriting once more to capture what had eluded me for two and a half years, a full-bodied character in the man.

Fonda was returning to Europe the next week for the entire summer. I worked on first-act revisions for several days, then phoned Fred's agent; I asked her to see whether Fonda would be willing to read the first act aloud to me with Annie, who was again in the east. I had three purposes in mind: to send Fonda off with more of me to think about, to hear my own work objectively in others' voices, and to clear Annie with Fonda, in the face of renewed inchings on the coast towards the singing dancer who was a bigger name. The agent had her doubts that Fonda would assent to a reading, but called back a few hours later to say she "couldn't believe it," he would be "delighted."

Accordingly, two breaths before Fonda's departure for Europe, he, Annie, and I met in his home, with Annie under instructions to vamoose the instant the act was read. But Fonda upset this conspiracy by asking Annie after the first act could she stay long enough to read the second?—and after the second, the third. I thus had a private preview of the entire play. Fonda read detachedly, and Annie read beautifully; what was more embarrassing, Fonda read seldom and Annie interminably. Nothing could have borne in upon me so uncomfortably the inequality of the roles as hanging thus on the spectacle of this renowned star, wearing horn-rimmed glasses and lankily slumped on his couch, waiting patiently all afternoon for his next line, and each time coming up with a monosyllable. In the third act Fred's agent rang the doorbell, and at its conclusion Annie fled. Fonda at once said he thought Annie "wonderful, you couldn't ask for anyone better"; this approval assured us of her, if we could assure ourselves of him. We talked about the man's role for another hour, parted with the understanding that I would rewrite it over the summer, after which Fonda would say yes or no, and I drove glumly home. I was far from certain about both the casting and my ability to rewrite satisfactorily.

Added to which, a very successful producer at this time told Leah he had wanted to invest a large sum in the show but had recoiled from Annie; he had seen her onstage out west and would not put a cent into her, she was "lousy, stank, like a dead thing." I thought this was not a strong enough recommendation to pass on to Fred.

Instead, I wrote Leah I had to trust my own eyes and ears, it was what they were for, and—defiantly—I was more worried about Fonda than about Annie. I was more worried about both of them. To Fred and Arthur I wrote that what I really missed in the reading was the ironic bite essential to the man's part, and that if we were lucky enough to get Fonda he would present a directorial problem not to be underestimated. Having conveyed thus my lone conviction that we were in pursuit of a piece of miscasting, I joined the pursuit.

I unhappily put aside the novel. Ignoring Fonda's personal quality—good advice Fred's agent gave me—I defined the task as one of so writing the character that any actor would take pleasure in playing him; I began again on page one, and whenever the girl had more lines on a page than the man, I wrote more for the man; but the quantity had to come out of something, and the something coalesced—I hoped—as the man's innards. I lost my grumpiness, and worked away with zest. In the middle I received a long and brilliant letter from the playwright in Hollywood who had disliked the play, anatomizing from memory its problems, particularly the man, in a way that fell helpfully into place in my own thinking. June went, July went, August went, and by the second-act curtain I had added a half hour to the script solely in the man's lines. I now stopped to breathe, and Fred sent the two acts abroad to Fonda. After two weeks of silent hemorrhaging, and an air-mail inquiry to the wording of which Fred devoted a full day, a cable arrived from Fonda beginning, "Start it rolling, I am yours."

It had taken us twelve months to get two actors, and finally we had them, for better or worse.

6

THE moment Fonda said yes, the entire production sprang into being; at last I understood Leah's insistence on stars as a necessity in the economics of show business, we rubbed the name Fonda like Aladdin's lamp and what was not, was. But our business structure reared up out of the lamp more or less behind my back, which was still bent over the third act. It was initiated by Fred and his lawyer; my own account is largely hearsay, and does no justice to its protracted complexities.

In the beginning was Joey Harris, an old campaigner of thirty who consented (I mean was not simply hired: from Fonda down all our employees took the script home, passed on its merits, and debated with their wives whether to tie the family fortunes to it) to be our company manager. Joey's job was to establish and run the business end of the show, from laying out the initial budget to accounting for the last ticket sold on Broadway soil. Joey budgeted the production at $80,000, divided into fifty units of $1,600 each. To raise this was the next chore, but the sine qua non was Fonda's signature on a contract.

All the principal contracts—negotiated by a hive of lawyers and agents—were as laboriously arrived at as mine had been a year earlier. The one with Henry, known to the profession and hereinafter as Hank, took weeks to settle: he ended up owning

25 per cent of the show by investing $20,000 in it personally; he was guaranteed a salary of $2,500 weekly against an ultimate 15 per cent of the box-office gross, which in a capacity week would bring him more than $4,500; and he could leave for more lucrative work after six months. Annie's contract was barer: she was to receive $550 weekly, could be held for two years if she was the success we hoped, or fired prior to the fifth out-of-town performance if she was not, and her second and third half-years would each be enlivened by a $100 raise. Arthur as director received a $3,500 fee and 2.5 per cent of the box office, which in a capacity week would amount to better than $700; in addition he was to enjoy 5 per cent of the production's profits, which would be zero until the $80,000 was paid off. I as author cost the show nothing in cash beyond my advance, unless my opus brought the entire $80,000 down in ruins around us; otherwise my royalty in a capacity week would come to something in excess of $2,500.

The $60,000 still remaining was raised by a single letter which Joey mailed out to a list of prospective backers, chiefly provided by Fred. The letter stated we had Fonda under contract, enclosed an application for the purchase of units, and suggested a blithe check in reply. The response to Hank's name was so instantaneous that Joey said it "set some kind of a world's record"; we were now a "hot property," within a week or two we were oversubscribed, units had to be rationed, money returned, and tardy friends placated. We ended up with thirty-nine privileged angels, an unusually low number. The first box-office receipts—minus weekly operating costs, the percentages "off the top," and monies reserved for a sinking fund—would go entirely to these backers, until their investment was repaid; thereafter profits would be divided, half to the backers and half to the producer, whose share in a capacity week would then approximate $4,000. (This standard fifty-fifty arrangement was in this instance somewhat complicated by Hank's deal as one fourth owner.) Fred and Hank and the backers also would divide 40 per cent of my receipts from movie, radio, TV, second-class touring, stock, amateur, and foreign rights.

While these bargainings were in process, Joey was also negotiating for a theater in New York and pre-Broadway bookings out of town. Here again our troubles evaporated under Hank's name; one businessman who made concessions to Joey said, "That star and that script, I got a hard-on for that show"—though when Joey pressed for more he added, "But it's not *that* big"—and late in the season as we were, we found ourselves not only with good theaters in Washington and Philadelphia, but with a New York plum. This was the Booth Theatre, the most intimate house on Broadway, so favorable for a two-character play that we had lusted after it for a year. The details of this contract, said by Joey to be one of the most benign ever conceded, were manifold: they included arranging with the show then in occupancy to vacate, a rental of 25 per cent of our box office—in a capacity week more than $7,500—and the famous "stop clause," whereby if our receipts in two consecutive weeks fell below $15,000 we were evictable.

Simultaneously, other talents, services, and equipment were being contracted for. We rented a theater to rehearse in. We engaged a set designer, a press agent, three stage managers, two understudies, a costume "finder," a master crew—electrician, carpenter, prop man—and a noted artist, for a drawing to be used in ads and posters. All these and other commitments were being juggled in mid-air at once; none of them could be made obligatory upon Fred till the money was raised; the money could not be raised till Hank's contract was in and Hank's contract could not be assumed till the money was in, but by some act of prestidigitation everything was wrapped up in a single moment, and we were ready to roll. Hank's position as kingbolt in this vehicle was attested to not only by his share of the take, but by the fact that Fred insured his life for $225,000; no one else in the production had a cash value to us, dead or alive.

Our production costs, as finally audited, with a short story, play, or novel hidden in every item, appeared thus:

Scenery		
Designing	$ 4,000.00	
Painting and building scenery	21,750.93	
		$25,750.93
Props purchases and rentals		2,895.30
Costumes		1,318.77
Electrical and sound equipment		1,183.08
Director—advance fee		3,500.00
Author—advance fee		3,000.00
Rehearsal expenses		
Salaries:		
Cast	$ 1,039.84	
Stage Managers	2,410.90	
Production secretary	218.56	
Crew	1,822.50	
Wardrobe	122.92	
Theater expense and rent	1,463.50	
Script expense	532.19	
Telephone and administrative expense	527.20	
		8,137.61
Preliminary advertising		
Press agent salary and expense	$ 1,193.26	
Newspaper advertising	7,366.59	
Photos and signs	1,134.98	
Subscription service, Theatre Guild	245.00	
		9,939.83

Opening Nite expense	$ 636.15
Stagehands	6,811.26
Company manager	2,275.00
Office expense	1,250.00
Legal fees and disbursements	2,174.93
Legal advertising	619.50
Auditing fees	409.75
Railroad transportation	800.86
Payroll taxes	334.37
Carting	1,559.58
Insurance	1,305.64
Blue Cross and Health Insurance Plan	276.82
TOTAL PRODUCTION COSTS	$74,179.38

These costs were those of getting the show "mounted"; they did not include the subsequent weekly operating expenses, which were to be met out of box-office receipts, if any. If insufficient, the show would close.

In all this I was reminded of a different Aladdin's lamp. Once upon a time, a memory of an episode in the real world of years ago had begun to worm around in my head. The memory was unreal as any shadow of an echo; but it drew to itself other memories, of deeds and wishes, mental bric-a-brac from obscure corners of time and place, and when these—in that moment of incandescence which is a writer's godsend—sprang into a coherent image, I wrote a play; that is, I gave those shadows a harmless kind of paper reality. But now they were re-entering life in the material world, and on their account scores of persons I had never heard of were engaged in doings as actual as the initial episode; it had secretly become part of their reality, and because of it their lives would never be quite the same again. It was a strange, if not particularly modest, thought.

ACT TWO

September–December 1957

In what follows, I must ask the reader to keep in mind certain materials already given; events marched inexorably out of them. Though I mean this to be as objective a ledger of a complex operation as one participant can balance, it is also a personal history, still a licking of wounds, in which may be found lurking as many grains of salt as readers should take any self-image with. Allowance thus being made for parallax, I will tabulate our given materials as:

One, I had written a two-character play in which the man's role was deficient. Two, this role had been declined by a dozen stars, and production of the play without one seemed to me tottering on the brink of abandonment; it was rescued by Hank. Three, in my view Hank's style, which I respected, and that of the role, in those attributes where it had my respect, were not compatible; their marriage was one to which I had given a reluctant blessing on the brink. Four, our casting was inverted: the starry role was to be played by an unknown, the mundane role by the star. Five, Arthur as director in a maiden effort had to cope with and mediate between two older men: a star who had been one for thirty of Arthur's thirty-five years, and an author who under a layer of reasonableness had devoted an obstinate quarter of a century to an avoidance of collaborators.

I stress this avoidance as an item because in what here purports to be a portrait of a collaborative medium, warts and all, my eye was hypnotically attracted to the warts. I never thought that these were more numerous than in other productions—more likely less: fewer people, fewer warts—but I was not a real playwright, bred in and devoted to show business, who could swallow them without blinking. I had precedent loves in literary forms, where the warts I was used to were solely my own; my eye saw what it saw, but undimmed by custom and impressionable by novelty; my appraisals and reactions were never those of an insider.

Months later I was asked, well, what would I have changed? and looking back upon these givens, I saw nothing alterable. At one point, in mid-December, I girded my loins to alter everything; what this opened up in me was a vulnerability I had never experienced in my forty-three years; but the intent was short-circuited, and even that was ineludible.

8

Two months of waiting had set in, for rehearsals to make all our dreams and nightmares come true. The earliest we could get into the Booth Theatre was January 12, 1958. Our entire schedule was set up to meet this date: we were to begin rehearsals on November 4, open in Washington on December 5, open in Philadelphia on December 25, move to New York to play two paid previews on January 14 and 15, and bare our breasts to the official firing squad, seven newspaper critics, on January 16.

The fixing of this date cost me something between $4,500 and $45,000. I was under contract to report to a studio in Hollywood on December 1, to do a screenplay for a sum which depended on whether the contract ran its minimal or maximal period; I wrote them I could not report until late January, and was fired by airmail. I had in hand the income from the book of my TV play, *The Miracle Worker*, which was published in August, looked more real to me between covers than the telecast to thirty million spectators, and sold nine hundred copies; it was a top-secret publication. Meanwhile I made use of September and October to begin a stage version of it, and to finish rewriting *Two for the Seesaw*.

Fred and Arthur had returned from the coast, and in October I made two trips to the city, partly to confer on the script with them, but chiefly to look at the preliminary sketches of the set. The action took place in two unconnected flats, the girl's and the man's; our designer, George Jenkins, in talks with Fred and Arthur, had conceived these as separable and doubly mobile, riding on tracks onstage and off, and each on its own turntable swinging to present various views of itself from scene to scene. This inventive design would not only deliver the significant acting areas downstage as wanted, but multiply the visual possibilities of a show which, with a limited supply of actors, needed every element of variety we could get into it. My sole qualm, when we saw the sketches in George's apartment-workroom, had to do with the decor: the man's room looked like Raskolnikov's, and the girl's was as smart as a Mondrian. I asked for a style of cluttered mishmosh in the girl's, and George agreed to have a new color sketch ready the following week; when I next saw it, the decor seemed more consonant with my character.

I also felt, in the interests of aural variety, we should have snatches of music covering the scene changes. But by union fiat these had to be live, not recorded, which in salaries would cost us a minimum of $135 a week per musician, or $500 to $1,000 weekly; this was standard. Arthur suggested we use city sounds instead, recorded, at $51 weekly. The musicians thus went unemployed; this also was standard.

Hank now was back in his New York home, and Fred convoyed Arthur there to be introduced. Arthur reported Hank was "charming," had quoted his family as "loving the play," and when asked what if any reservations he still had—the implication was for rewriting—had ventured two: the girl's profanity might be toned down, and a couple of lines the man spoke aloud to himself Hank doubted he could deliver, since he personally did not talk aloud to himself. We agreed it took courage for Hank to do the play at all, let alone put his reputation in the hands of such green schnooks, of whom he demanded so little; I thought that for a star of his magnitude to be so reasonable was fairly unreasonable.

Arthur and I whittled away at the script, which was overlong. This was a judgment made in terms not solely of content, but of theatergoing habits: if we raised the curtain before eight-forty the first act would be invaded by late-comers, and if we brought it down later than eleven the third would be shattered by commuters running out to catch trains. Even without this uncooperative attitude of the public, the form seemed constrictive to me; my reason for not bringing in a third character was that I already lacked room for two. Nevertheless we cut, without screams, a pound of flesh here, a pound of flesh there.

In our first session we tangled over an item trivial in itself, but with reverberations fore and aft. In the initial act my two characters launched upon an optimistic affair; the curtain fell on the man somberly reading a telegram from his estranged wife. Arthur revived a suggestion of Fred's—I had vetoed it before—to minimize the telegram by moving it to the start of the scene, and to dedicate the curtain to the buoyancy of the affair. A somber curtain being exactly what I meant and wanted, to foreshadow the end of the play, I balked. The debate on this detail tensed up, went on for three vexing hours, and arrived nowhere. The strategic position of the telegram in itself was not our topic; our subterranean dispute was the play throughout, and the degree of commitment my man, internally committed to his marriage, could make to a transient affair. Arthur in preceding months had persistently tugged for more, and I had resisted. In this I was arguing for what I knew was psychological veracity, and Arthur I thought for the dramatic richness of the relationship onstage; these were two different realities. Arthur said he did not want to "corrupt" my play, and I went back to Massachusetts already sick of this loquacious medium in which I was to adjust my material to others' views because they could not work with conviction out of mine. In our next session the point was tacitly surrendered my way, but it was to hound me thereafter.

Arthur and his wife phoned on the weekend prior to rehearsals and the families exchanged jocularities about our respective panics. The business forecast he reported was good: theater parties—of organizations who raise funds by buying the entire house and selling tickets to their members at a stiff markup, making for a full but sulky audience—had rallied to us at the first news of Hank's signing, and someone's estimate, it hardly mattered whose, was that our advance sale would hit $350,000. It seemed that come the worst, by the grace of Henry Fonda we would all eat in 1958.

On Sunday evening November 3 I boarded the New York train, leaving my older boy sobbing in his mother's hand on the platform. I assumed I was seated in an everyday coach of our limping local; I did not know I had entered a sealed spaceship in which, divorced from family, ties to earth, and nightly sleep, I was to be shot to the moon.

9

I REPORTED at ten o'clock the next morning to a handsome wood-paneled room atop a 57th Street building, where we were to rehearse the first week; here I found, standing or seated around a long table, Fred, Arthur, Hank, Annie, Leah, and two young men equipped with coffee, pads, pencils, innumerable cough drops, and aspirin for all, who turned out to be not vendors but our stage managers.

Hank and Annie were the two I was eager to dote on, almost as though I had written them into flesh. But exchanging some small talk with Hank about our respective summers I again sensed a deficiency of contact between us, in more than that he failed to smile at my jokes. Annie however was all jokes. ("My real name's Italiano—you know, it means Italian in Italian?") She had gained thirty pounds over the summer, which I had not written, and an astonishing output of tresses as well, adorning her nape; I blinked later when she removed it with one hand, I saw I was really in the land of make-believe. The thirty pounds took longer.

The first morning was spent in listening to the two of them read the play through; the only difference from the June reading for me was that now Hank had much more rhetoric to get his tongue around. But I told myself we were rich in time: in view of the length of the roles, both actors, at Fred's request, had consented to an additional week of rehearsal; rehearsal pay was only $65 a week, and the extra week—at $100—had required the consent also of Equity, the actors' union. We read the play a second time after lunch, introducing the cuts Arthur and I had made, and commenced to talk about meanings. It did not add to my security when an Equity representative appeared out of the wood-paneling with a membership application for Annie to sign, as a nonunion beginner. The work day ended at six, and I went home with Arthur for dinner, where we congratulated ourselves on knowing how to start rehearsals.

The second day was similar, except that we were minus Leah—she had come only for my baptismal reading—and much of the time Fred, who for the next month drifted in and out like a man who had built a juggernaut and could not find a seat on it. The procedure, which we were to observe all week, was for Hank and Annie to read a scene; Arthur then discussed its meanings and tones with them, breaking it down into separate chunks, passages within these, and isolated lines; when these were presumably understood the scene was read again, and was supposed to grow in richness and conviction. I sat away from the table, in silence, unless questions were put directly to me or Arthur took off on a tack contrary to my purport, which happened, but seldom; it was surprising in what detail he perceived my intent. In the afternoon we clocked a complete reading. We were still at least twenty minutes overlong; in a script of one hundred twenty pages, this meant one page of every six had to come out. I accompanied Arthur home again that afternoon, and we resumed our surgery.

In the evening I escorted a friend to see a hit play, and was as usual impatient with the doings onstage; the truth was, it had been several years since I had taken a believing interest in the theater. My present involvement, after twenty years of dreamwork, bore out one of the life-slogans I held: everything comes to him who waits, too late.

The third day of readings, which by now were affecting my buttocks, was varied somewhat by two visitors. Our press agent brought in publicity photos of Hank and Annie in her detachable hair and a layout for our advance Washington ad, which lent an unreal air of reality to our undertaking; George Jenkins brought in a set model, and discussed with the actors the alleged spots where they could make costume changes while the sets were whirling around. Two other happenings marked this day. The first was Hank's reaction to my explanation of some lines about the man's marital infidelities prior to the time of the play; he said quickly, "Oh, I don't want the part!" The second was Arthur's leading Annie into the meaning of the third act, which baffled her; he gave her no answers, but by patient socratic questioning let her make discovery after exciting discovery on her own.

Up to this point it was Annie's inquiries that pre-empted each day, and she and Arthur were having in effect a tête-à-tête; Hank sat as a spectator, with a fixed tolerant smile. On the fourth day I changed chairs, to watch his face instead of the back of his head. I noted that when he had a question it was invariably about objective "business"—would he be standing or sitting on this speech, how could he get to the phone if he was at the window—whereas Annie's questions were altogether about the girl's inner life. Hank was fifty-two years old, and Annie twenty-six; they were of different generations, not only personally, but of the country's total culture and of its theater in specific; Hank like me had come out of a less introspective tradition, which I thought I understood, and was a stony witness of the Freudian and Stanislavskian currents that Arthur and Annie inhabited as naturally as fishes. I felt we were in danger of neglecting Hank, and having said so to Arthur, I took the evening train home to my other neglectees.

In the morning I bundled wife and children and 107 toys into the station wagon and drove back to the city, where I caught the afternoon rehearsal; I joined Arthur in extending questions and comments to Hank. Arthur stepped these up on the sixth day, and it cost us the tolerant smile. The character as we dug into it perplexed and troubled Hank, particularly in its unpleasant aspects, and lines which at his request I had retained in the rewriting I now learned he had taken literally one way, not ironically two. Since every third line of the man's had an ironic duplicity, much of the character was in the nature of an unwelcome surprise to him. In this climate of mutual dissatisfaction, our discussions grew more and more painful, especially to my buttocks. I privately apologized to Arthur for talking so much, but he said it in no way superseded his function, since my explaining effected no change in Hank's readings; and at the end of the day he left the meaning of one sentence hanging, for Hank to ponder through on his own overnight. We separated in a general gloom.

The next day was Sunday, and Arthur had scheduled an afternoon rehearsal. However, our cherubs were progressively wrecking the apartment we were in, each other, and their haggard mother, so I bundled wife and children and 112 toys into the station wagon and drove back to the hills, from whence cometh our part-time help. In the evening Arthur phoned happily to say it had worked, Hank had come in clear about the sentence and much looser.

I drove out of the hills at dawn and into the city at nine-thirty, had a second breakfast, and reported for our eighth day; we were still around the table, in danger of disappearing under it, while we waited for our rehearsal stage to be vacated by another production. Hank did seem to me lighter in the morning—we were coming to hover over his state of mind like two anxious hawks—but not much looser. After lunch he again became unhappy with himself and the lines. It was evident by now that the self-mocking irony I intended in my man would not be in the show; when Hank honestly labored for my rhetoric, what came out hurt his ear as much as mine. This hurt was not to be dissipated by talk, but we talked, with no other choice and no result except tension. My resolution not to smoke during the rehearsal period now broke down, and I bummed my first cigarette from Pete Van Zandt, the stage manager. Still, I thought I was resigned to certain compromises—I had lived with the prospect since June—and I wanted the show to work on its feet, not on the page; so before we disbanded I asked Arthur in a note to assure Hank we would not let him go onstage with one line unrewritten that he felt uncomfortable or untruthful with. This was a promise I meant to keep, but I misjudged its scope. When Arthur took Hank aside I took Annie aside; I told her that, while she would not be receiving too many compliments out loud, I could not name another actress I would rather see in the part. These messages in contrary motion given, Arthur and I took ourselves to his apartment for dinner, where we diverted his pregnant wife with our own labor pains to bring my man forth; Arthur said in woe, "I've used up all my directorial wiles!" In truth, we were both quite troubled. I drove back into Stockbridge at midnight, a long day, seven hours at the wheel and eight at the forceps.

The ninth day was our first without rehearsal. It was no holiday, though; I spent half of it in the studio, cutting the third act and simplifying speeches of the man's, as promised.

With the dawn came my birthday, so I bought myself a ticket to New York, where Hank made me another present. This was our first day on a stage, in a 42nd Street rooftop theater used for private shows a generation earlier by Flo Ziegfeld and in which the air had not been changed since; but when I entered with my suitcase in hand and saw Hank walking about onstage, I had no nose for anything else. His figure commanded the entire playing area. For a year I had been listening to Leah talk about "star quality," a favorite term in the theater which to me signified nothing but a religious respect for the golden calf, including some cows I could name; now I saw it incarnate, any body that stood near Hank's shrank in interest. Arthur said with some admiration, "He stalks that stage like a stallion." Also present, for the first time, were our two stand-bys—an elevated term for understudies—Gaby Rodgers and Kevin McCarthy, whom I sat down behind in the sixth or seventh row; Gaby with her eyes on Hank murmured he was "the most elegant man" she ever saw, and Kevin said that watching him he knew what "physical envy" was, at "simply how that mass moves through space, almost always interestingly."

Arthur and Pete had devised a plan for rehearsing upon two white tarpaulins, which saved us many subsequent headaches with the actors and set. These tarpaulins duplicated the floor space of the two turntables on which the sets would ride, and were not only ruled into appropriate areas—kitchen, bed, steps—but could be turned by hand from scene to scene to match the action of the tables. Upon these tarps were set makeshift boxes, stools, and other odds and ends to represent furniture; the actors were not to make the acquaintance of the genuine articles, however different or confusing, until dress rehearsal in Washington. This was standard insanity, necessitated by a union rule that if true furniture were used true stagehands had to be present to move it, price, another thousand dollars weekly. Instances have been rumored of producers smuggling into rehearsal certain indispensable pieces of the final furniture, but we never did anything like that. As we moved out of one scene into another, Pete and his two assistants would rush to drag one tarpful of furnishings offstage and the other on, tugging it into position clockwise and counterclockwise as marked; three weeks of this turned their knuckles bulgy with calluses.

Arthur was now ready to "block" the show, that is, establish the moves—stand here, cross on this line, sit on that—of the actors. He did this not by paper plan, but by letting Hank's and Annie's impulses dictate their actions, which he then sharpened, contradicted, or elaborated. Half of this movement was obligatory and already written into the script, since I cannot write scenes without simultaneously impersonating the actors and director; the rest of it was created by the three of them on their feet, with occasional outcries of pleasure and pain from me. In this way we blocked two scenes that day. Annie, onstage for the first time in her career, was the converse of Hank, considerably dimmer than around the table, her body unsure of itself, of the character, of the playing space. Arthur had predicted that the new phase of work would be advantageous for Hank, disadvantageous for Annie, and it seemed that our labors lay in the direction of meanings for one and movements for the other. Nevertheless, the two scenes looked promising.

At the end of the day Annie gazed around at the stage barren and bright under the worklights, the stage manager's desk offside on the proscenium, the director's spartan chair down center, the producer conferring in the wings with the publicity agent, and the audience seats in a gloom, populated by a solitary author; she said, "It's just like it is in the movies!" Arthur said, "How else do you think we learn how to do it?"

I phoned Leah that evening to say Hank's presence onstage was wonderful; she was delighted to hear me so affirmative after fourteen months. The affirmation ran into quicksand the following afternoon, when Hank exclaimed my man had "too many complexes, I can't follow this guy!" Hank's unhappiness with the role brought activity to a standstill; Annie would lie down on a cot, while Arthur squatted close to Hank onstage in hour-long sotto voce talks which I tried both to overhear and overlook from the seats. One of our agents sat in on rehearsal that day, watched Annie work, and chilled me by whispering it was good we had Gaby in reserve in case we "wanted a change." Annie was in fact improving, but it was altogether a depressing day. I devoted part of the night to a documentary movie about a bullfighter, throughout which I tried to convince myself that Arthur was being paid to stab our bull, not I; Arthur told me he devoted all of the night to lying awake.

I missed the twelfth morning, which I spent instead over coffee in a hotel suite with Leah and a movie producer. The producer was interested in dissuading me from making a stage play of *The Miracle Worker*, so that we might collaborate on a movie of it; I was pleased, but I had already turned down one movie sale because I thought the casting it entailed would falsify the piece, and I was having enough trouble with collaborators in the family morass of the theater without taking on also the technological morass of the movie industry. I went back with Leah to rehearsal, where she had her first glimpse of Annie in action, still improving. It was a dinner scene, and Leah presently said, "When you're that young and pretty, even chewing is attractive"; she thought Annie "quite interesting," but that Arthur and I must "spice up" Hank's performance. That afternoon Annie was confused about the inner logic of a passage and with Arthur's prompt agreement went through it improvising her own lines in lieu of mine, exploring the emotional content under them; but Hank would not improvise back, he responded firmly with my exact words like a shield; the moment contained in miniature two generations of acting approach. We now had four scenes blocked. Hank's mood was up again, and he had objections only to a spot in which the man was reluctant to accept a job.

I went home with Arthur, and after dinner we sat for a moment to this spot. We staggered to our feet at two o'clock in the morning; the half-dozen lines had led us into our old controversy, and back and forth across the entire play. Arthur thought the man should welcome the job, generously, for the girl; I said commitment to his prior marriage must hamstring him in making a new life. The larger fact again was that the man was not written with the authority of full-fleshed individuality which would have precluded—as it did in the case of the girl—debate on what he "should" do. I had been hit by so much criticism of him over two years now that I was vulnerable to every objection and anxious to put still more meat on him; but when Arthur questioned whether he "had a right" to say this or do that, I replied of course he had no right but it was in character; unsure as I was, I knew that individuation did not lie in the direction of a general moral ideal. Fundamentally, the choice emerging was between a "sympathetic character" and one with involutions that the director was not attracted to, the actor would not play, and audiences allegedly would not watch. Arthur said troubledly he felt the material had "an organic life of its own" that he was "tampering with," my feeling exactly, and we fell into our respective beds with nothing to show for five hours of brilliant conversation except three unbrilliant lines. They were, however, sympathetic.

The thirteenth day was satisfactorily uneventful. We blocked in the rest of the second act; under Arthur's velvet hand Annie was taking to the stage now like a puppy to a meadow, and many moments of Hank's were improving, though I felt deprived of the character I intended. I traveled home by train that night, for a Sunday with my family, and left my script in the theater to avoid it.

I thus missed another session with Hank, which Arthur recounted when I came in on Monday. Hank had asserted he could not act it "our way," he had to do it "his way"; Arthur told me it was much better. But when we now ran the first two acts without interruption, what struck my eye was how much of what I conceived as the play's innards was not on the stage. The three lines I had yielded came back to offend me as slickly amiable, but of a piece with the level of performance throughout; the darker material was not being acted, and I departed to stew that evening over Arthur's saying the show needed more "finesse." I believed it needed more bowels.

I told Arthur the next morning I thought it "slickly amiable." Though a bit taken aback, he listened attentively, as always; he said Hank at present was "overextended," therefore anxious, and must be allowed more "success" before we asked for more depth. I questioned whether these were separately achievable, but I was not directing the show, except at three o'clock in the morning. That noon Kevin took me to a work session at the Actors Studio, the fountainhead of Stanislavskian method in this country, where Lee Strasberg discoursed to two actors onstage, a tape recorder at his side, and a roomful behind him, on truth and human fullness in acting; I sat rapt. We went back to the actual theater as though from church to a gambling den. I came in on Hank again objecting to my man's "bad character," he had "an ungovernable temper" and was in other ways "nasty" and "ugly"; I was not bulletproof against this criticism, which lodged in the pit of my stomach next to my hunger for a view of the other qualities I believed I had written into the character. Hank also felt that Arthur had him "moving" too much, in a scene the intended point of which was that the man blew in like a windstorm, did six things simultaneously, and blew out. I asked Kevin and Gaby—who as stand-bys had their own gloom, they had been spectators for a week now without an eye to work for—if I might listen to them read the next day.

In the evening I visited a painter's studio, and envied her; she was working in a medium where she alone could ruin it. This seemed to me a definition of art. I had never given workers in the secondary arts their due—before rehearsals I wrote a friend he would not be hearing from me unless he read my obituary in *Variety* under the heading Killed By Actors—and when another artist asked what I had against actors, I said writing for them was like painting not in oils but in colored mice; after the painting was finished the mice began running around. It was dawning on me that I was perhaps not a theater man.

On the seventeenth morning we blocked in the remainder of the third act. I lunched with Joey Harris, who told me something of his contrapuntal doings, and afterwards I went careening by taxi with him and Fred into the wilds of Brooklyn. Our set was being built there in a bedlam of a workshop as big as a ball park, one of several that had bid on the job. Low bid had been $19,000; as I inspected the girl's multi-levelled room I thought it looked like every cent of it, and wondered where my impoverished urchin had gotten the $19,000. We careened back to the theater. Gaby and Kevin, for lack of a room to rehearse in, were reading a scene in a corner of the lobby; I listened to them for an hour while the rehearsal inside broke up, answered some questions, and then went in to pester

Arthur with my doubts about the girl's room. He was too edgy to attend to them, and at dinner with him I learned why: it had been a sour afternoon, and Hank had lingered after rehearsal to object to Annie's performance as too emotional.

The next day the elevator boy who carried us up to the theater asked me if I thought we had a hit. I said who knew. He said he had watched us rehearse, and added thoughtfully, "Not very convincing." I said, "Oh?" He said, "I dunno, you should see more anger in his face or something." I said I would inform the director.

Actually I did, not only as a joke. Arthur was as glum as I had yet seen him, but Hank reported in gayer spirits. A new employee came aboard during the day, a girl named Jessica Levy, whose job as production secretary was to take notes, retype pages, and be anybody's factotum; being green—old hands like Pete and Joey were opinionless as mummies—she ventured a criticism, and after watching Hank and Annie in a third-act scene told me she "believed him more than her." It was understandable: Annie was now feeling her powers and commencing to overplay.

I went to Stockbridge by train that evening, to see if my family were still there; they were, but I wasn't, our house was taking on the unreality of a stage set, and in the real world I was married to Hank. Late the next afternoon I drove to New York with my wife, the country one, and the elevator boy left his car to pursue us with his counsel down the hall, calling out his final warning, "This part isn't for Mr. Fonda, Hurd Hatfield would have been better!" My hand was on the theater door, and I said, "Sssh." "Oh," he said, "I wouldn't hurt his feelings for the world." We stepped inside, where Arthur was onstage talking to Hank, and the first words we heard out of Hank were, "Well, if *that* doesn't show, maybe I should be replaced in the part."

The pressure was hardening. We had one week of rehearsal left, at the end of which we were to give two run-throughs—

performances without sets, lights, or costumes—for invited audiences. The five of us were carrying the production like a bagful of assorted velocities, this way and that in five directions, each signposted success; more truthfully, it was carrying us, in one inexorable direction no one had chosen to go. Fred's state of mind I was still not in touch with. His body was temporarily in California, to supervise a TV broadcast of a stage musical; word came back on the day of performance they had moved the stage sets into the studio, and found they had no room left for the cameras. Of the four of us in 42nd Street, the least troubled it seemed was our neophyte, Annie. Her worry was control: she worked so subjectively out of instinct that external comments of not enough or too much did little except to bewilder her. I thought her work not only authentically created my girl in the flesh, but often—my first such experience with an actor—transcended the lines with a humor or poignancy I had not suspected in them; but no one, including herself, knew what facing a live audience would do to her. Hank was the only old pro in the setup, and I knew he would do exactly what he was rehearsing. Leah and Fred's agent, who had been most eager in signing him, assured me he would "come through" when he had an audience. This was an article of theatrical faith I had often heard of and never seen any evidence for; my own belief was that what I had written was alien to him as man and actor, and I could not see where the qualities I wanted were to come from. The remedy of rewriting the character to fit the actor meant wrecking the structure of the play; it turned upon the very moments Hank most disliked. Arthur's worries were too multiple to keep track of, from small sound-effects offstage to large ones onstage from author and star that the whole show was respectively too light and too dark. I was most happy with the inventiveness he brought to the staging, which in the comic moments especially outran the writing, but a problem in my view was his relationship with Hank: with all the talk it was essentially not communicative. Also, Arthur was still obdurately protecting the language of the script. Hank's worry was perhaps the worst. He had contracted to do a play about "two charming people," and one of them now was being called upon to shout, weep, strike a girl, be weak, selfish, mocking, and do other uncharming things that his flesh rebelled against; he walked away from Arthur's compliments in silence, until at last he said vexedly, "I don't want to be *told* it's good, I have to *feel* it's good." The dilemma was that his authentic stage presence, simplicity, attractiveness, emotional reticence, had little to do with the character as I conceived it and disappeared when he struggled to be what we asked, so we had neither. Jessica on her second day changed her mind about believing him more than Annie. But on several counts I thought we were favoring Annie, willy-nilly: of the two characters she was playing the one that stimulated the director to richer invention, as undeniably it had the author; she was temperamentally unremote, whereas Hank when the four of us walked to lunch instinctively drifted out to the curb or a few long paces ahead of us; and as a performer she was more responsive to Arthur and the interior imagery of his direction. Night after night Hank was working doggedly on the lines at home, with one of the stage managers on hand to cue him. He was coming to think that, while the part "read beautifully," it was too "internal" to be acted, though he had to perform it before his public a week hence; it was a star's nightmare. Yet when he kicked up it was never any outraged stardust, he tugged the tarpaulins around like the rest of us when necessary, and his desperation was that of a hardworking honorable man, in trouble. So were we all, all honorable men, and in trouble.

I was my usual philosophical self, that is, in a black wrath of impotence.

The twenty-first day was a Sunday, rehearsal as usual—the company worked nine Sundays in a string—but commencing at noon. When my wife and I stepped in this time, we saw Hank challenging Arthur onstage about a scene he felt was being directed too heavily for "unconscious" meanings in the girl; Hank's voice lifted, "It doesn't play, it doesn't *go*, I know this as well as I know anything in my life! I wish I could show you how, boy!" Arthur after a silence said, "Show me how," and Hank paced through the scene with a go that delivered my lines but not their internal intent.

This contretemps overhung the entire afternoon, except for one moment. Arthur's wife and mine watching another scene were moved to tears, and at its conclusion I climbed onstage, went over to Hank—he was sitting silent and alone on a cot—and said, "Hank, most of this is dreadful," and his face lit up, in the first minute of genuine contact I ever felt between us; I privately ascribed it to an honest statement, and added that the scene could not be as bad as I thought, because our wives were out there in tears. We broke for food in the late afternoon. Arthur then banished his wife and mine, and on our return to the theater, invited me onstage for a conference to clear the air.

We talked the first act through. What I missed most in the performance was the emotional zigzag I had written; the mood was rarely linear, in every passage I meant the dialogue to make abrupt jumps, from jokes to griefs to jokes to hostilities. From my point of view, these jumps constituted the textural concept of the play, and were essential to avoid the monotony of the two characters. From Hank's point of view, they were unfollowable and unactable. It hardly mattered whose metabolism was in the right, I had no hope by now of seeing mine onstage in Hank's flesh, indeed this combination was often not better than nothing, but worse; and I made rewrite notes on some of the jumps and obliquities that both of us were, for different reasons, unhappy with. When my man for instance spoke with self-mockery about lacking a radio, he was in my view speaking about his total loneliness; Hank objected that the audience would interpret this in him as self-pity at lacking a radio. That in fact was what appeared onstage, and I made a note to take out the radio and substitute a straightforward speech of loneliness. On the other hand, some of Hank's objections were to plain deficiencies in the writing. Here Arthur had been in the position of defending me when I should have been surrendered to the axe, so I surrendered myself, which charmed everyone, not excluding me. One such spot that troubled Hank concerned the man's motivation for staying in the girl's room; I said his chief motivation was that I needed him there for an important moment a page later, and solicited Hank's help as an actor in solving the difficulty. Although somewhat unilateral, these compromises seemed honest, reasonable, and productive. Arthur afterwards said he thought the session most helpful, I said he should not feel obliged to defend the script at its weak moments, and he said but his training had been that it was precisely in such moments the actor and director were called upon to be most creative. It was a pregnant observation, and one that in the weeks ahead I often recalled nostalgically.

The next morning we continued our conference through the second act, singling out passages of the man's for me to rewrite. Arthur then reblocked a scene I had criticized. During a break, while Hank and Arthur were engaged in a sotto voce conversation off to the side, Annie and I had another; she told me she thought the play was "all there" despite Hank's criticisms, and for the first time I broke ranks to let her in on my concern, which indeed it hardly took a Champollion to decipher. Arthur later told me that Hank had moved him by saying that what he had to give the public was naturalness and ease, which this part did not let him feel, and his nights were sleepless with worry. In all this there was an esthetic and personal honesty; Hank could not bear to deliver a line falsely, just as I never heard him utter a sociable insincerity to any of us; and this honesty was a palpable asset for the character. It was not without its constrictive aspect in his art.

After lunch we ran the play through. The first act lay on the stage as immovable as a dead whale. In the second act Hank outplayed Annie; she seemed rattled and repeatedly forgot lines—I wondered whether my confidences were responsible—while Hank was commencing to reconcile much of the material with his own style. Still, my agent watching the third act said to me, "What's his reaction to her saying she doesn't want to live alone?" I said, "*That's* his reaction." She said, "That's no reaction." I said, "Sue me."

I had planned to drive my wife home to our offspring that night, but I dispatched her alone by train and stayed in town, to rewrite the passages promised. I brought them in the next morning. In one of our telephone scenes Hank was now so relaxed and attractive that I went onstage to tell him so; at lunch too—often a conversational dust bowl—he was for the second day open and talkative, entertaining the table with reminiscences. In the afternoon we returned to the first act, and inserted the new material. This act contained a fight scene, which had never been played at the combative level I intended; Hank now acceded to my request, and acted it at top pitch. It was unfortunate. We then postulated it as a small lovers' spat, which Hank much preferred, and acted on that level it had charm. Arthur and I took a breath, it was our first inkling that the violent areas of the play might be solvable, simply by reducing their level.

The next day was our twenty-fourth; it was a week before our Washington opening, and by Equity contract we were now allowed twelve-hour rehearsals. We worked single scenes during the day, and in the evening had a trial run-through. It promised to be at least presentable for our invited audience two days later, and everyone felt cheerier. I drove home that night for Thanksgiving, broke down at midnight on the parkway, found my way to Peekskill, and reached Stockbridge in a rented car at five in the morning.

In New York they celebrated Thanksgiving by rehearsing, not happily, as I heard when I drove the rented car down on Friday for our first run-through. Our audience that afternoon was to consist of the companies of two musical-comedy hits. I was on needles; I knew the performers must be too, and much lonelier with it, and I could not see them face our first audience unblessed, so in the lunch break I went shopping, ate a frankfurter at Nedick's, and brought back two spiritual offerings, a fifth of Jack Daniel's for Hank and a box of Chanel soap—an item from the play—for Annie. She was darting around like a cricket, and kissed me; Hank I found seated in an offstage corner, and he gave me a wan smile of thanks. I then stood at the door, waiting for the bevy of heavenly beauties from the chorus lines to appear, but the only women to file in were the usual mortals. When the influx ceased I settled in a rear row with Fred, who had flown back from Hollywood; Arthur mounted the stage, welcomed the audience, named the play, author, and cast, said we were the only show in town with more stage managers than actors, explained the sets—still two cryptic tarpaulins laden with odds and ends, the draggings around of which our callused stage managers had rehearsed in private to the last irreducible second—and came down to join Fred and me. Hank walked onstage and sat in position, and the play began.

After the first scene I stopped worrying about Annie, no audience was ever going to throw her; Hank seemed in a retreat of distaste, from the audience and from the role. Annie forgot a few lines, Hank not a word. It went smoothly enough, but no one laughed; since the play was supposed to be very funny, this was somewhat disconcerting. Yet the spectators were quite attentive. In the middle of the performance the plumbers arrived to fix the toilets downstairs, bangings on pipes and shouts of mutual encouragement ensued, climaxed by the emergence from the nether regions of two of the damned with a ladder half a block long, which after a variety of marches and countermarches they finally wrestled out of our side door in view of all; Fred, Arthur, and I glared at them, but ours were the only heads that turned from the stage. At the close of the play there was moderate applause, neither actor reappeared for a bow, and the audience dribbled out.

It was less than a triumph. When I took leave of some relatives and friends, and went onstage, I found Hank seated in a black gloom ringed by Arthur, Annie, and Fred in satellite glooms; Hank felt it had been an unmitigated disaster from start to finish. Fred now took firm charge—my first glimpse of him in action—and insisted on going through the play scene by scene with Hank to isolate all his disaster areas; this scrutiny produced only half a dozen, several of which were already marked for me to rewrite. I laughed out loud at this, and even Hank smiled. We then disbanded, Fred bought the Penns and me dinner, and we adjourned to Arthur's to discuss restagings and rewritings. This confab broke up at one-thirty in the morning.

The twenty-seventh day began with my retiring to an upstairs make-up room to rewrite chunks of the man's in three different scenes, while other scenes were in rehearsal below. These make-up rooms were next to toilets—from which indeed they were almost indistinguishable, in every theater we occupied—and Annie en route stuck her head in to say hello; in the course of exchanging news on our respective progress she said she sensed a growing competitiveness in the stage work. I rewrote through a private lunch—sandwich, malted, and toilet aroma—and when I brought the pages downstairs I observed that Hank's mood was again up. I suddenly felt that the function of such glooms was to communicate with more eloquence than language permitted; when others darkened the communicant brightened, a point had been made, action would be taken; and from that instant on I left these moods to others. In the afternoon we rehearsed the new material for the run-through that evening.

Our audience on this occasion was sharper, young playwrights from the New Dramatists Committee and students and faculty of the American Theatre Wing; they laughed. I relaxed. It was altogether a more generous show—though Annie played too broadly, Hank came somewhat out of his retreat—and the response was much warmer throughout, the applause heavier, the actors this time took a curtain bow, and several friends predicted we would have a hit. All of us, including Hank, left the theater encouraged.

On this upbeat I said good-by to New York until our return in January. A rehearsal call was up for the next day, another Sunday, but I intended to spend it with my family; on Monday morning we were to board the train for Washington, whither our true sets and props were already in transit. Saturday night I drove the rented car back to Peekskill, picked up my own, and arrived in Stockbridge at three a.m. Fifteen hours later I was on the train again, headed for a six-weeks' rendezvous with still another, final, and most implacable collaborator, the paying audience.

10

OUR crew, the set designer, and two of our stage managers had preceded us to Washington, to work on the sets and lights; the remainder of the company—we had increased it by two "dressers" for Annie and Hank—traveled there in a plush swivel-chaired car on Monday, December 2. Our world premiere was scheduled for Thursday evening.

Two conferences took place on the train. The first was at my request, with Arthur, Annie, and Hank; I monologized on the performances—Annie's overplaying, Hank's underplaying—and the need to bring them to one level, and then on what I called the profile of the play, meaning its contour of emotional turning points, which I felt was especially lacking in the first act. I found this conference much more enjoyable than the second, which was with Arthur and Fred at their request, and concerned as usual rewriting. The chief area in question was our second-act curtain: there was a complexity of "beats" here which for me were psychologically inseparable, but theatrically the effect was one of clutter which impeded the movement towards the curtain. I agreed to some radical weeding. Each of us now was beginning to quote and reflect the criticisms of friends at our run-throughs, that is, audience opinion.

We detrained in Washington, rode to our hotel in a straggle of taxis crammed with limbs and luggage, and separated to our rooms. The hotel was small, tasteful, friendly, and catered to theater folk. In my room I found a narrow bed on which I could fit neither lengthwise nor sidewise, so the management dug a double bed out of some subterranean vault and moved it in, after which I felt more cooperative about the rewriting. My rent was nominally $9.50 a day—I received a special "theatrical rate" of $7.50—for a room which, though comfortable, had at its soul the impersonality of the pallid glassed prints which pepped up its walls; it became hideous only with continued inhabitancy. We were now living on the show. Standard expense allowance was $20 a day, which seemed a great deal until I saw how it melted daily, on rent, meals, laundry, taxis to and from the theater, and desperate long-distance calls to the purple hills of home. These out-of-town allowances alone cost the production about $3,500, and this for a two-actor cast.

As soon as we were unpacked, a few of us piled eagerly into a taxi for the theater and the esthetic experience of our set, now supposedly in place. What we walked into was chaos, the stage so choked with jigsaw pieces of illusion it was impossible to find one's way across, cables underfoot everywhere, flooring half laid, winches connected to nothing, walls on their backsides, doors and windows leaning on each other in exhaustion, and our designer George Jenkins—in whose head alone some orderly image existed—directing a horde of wearied carpenters and stagehands who had been on their feet since Sunday, through the night. It seemed there was "a problem." Leaving it to George, I took a taxi back to the hotel and my own jigsaw of the second-act curtain.

The problem here was one of architecture: the give and take of the two characters, whatever their other failings, was at least logically built, and when I took out one brick anywhere, other bricks fell out all over the play. From that night on, for the next six weeks I was scurrying from scene to scene in a frantic effort to thrust bricks back, somewhere.

I thrust enough back on this occasion to deliver the changes Tuesday morning to the actors, and Arthur and Fred, in Annie's room. Annie was simultaneously being interviewed by the Washington press, but we isolated time to read the new material, which was simpler, in fact so much simpler that Arthur asked me to put some of the complications back in. I retired again to my room, settling to work in a squat on my double bed. In the afternoon I unsquatted and took the new pages to the theater, where I found the actors back upon a tarpaulin on the inclined floor of the lobby. The stage was not yet usable; though the sets were assembled, their movements on the turntables were still being worked over and the lights hung. George had more than a hundred spotlights to clamp on pipes aloft and focus, each of which took ten minutes, so illumination alone entailed eighteen hours of work. These labors had now been going on without pause for three days and two nights, our stage managers were white with fatigue, and in the dark aisle I almost stepped upon the faces of two stagehands, sleeping on the floor; this was what outsiders called the glamour of the theater. I returned to the rehearsal of the new lines in the lobby. Here I sat out of the way on the staircase, and at Arthur's request grumpily rewrote half a page to make one line clearer; I was coming to detest this need for instant clarity—to my mind we invariably substituted one explicit meaning for three implicit ones—but I had contracted for it when I wrote a play in the first place.

We broke for dinner in a restaurant, then came back and took the stage, at last, for a run-through. It would more properly have been christened a creep-through: this was Annie's and Hank's first encounter with the actual sets, the stagehands' first encounter with the scenes in sequence, the electricians' first encounter with the actors in motion, and at every third line the play would groan to a standstill, while missing props were searched for, lights criticized and adjusted, and the sets reasoned with not to take the whole fornicating night. It was after the witching hour when we adjourned, still in the second act.

Meanwhile the box-office report was disappointing. Tickets had been available in Washington for two weeks, we had expected a $35,000 advance sale and done $16,000; we were to lose more than $15,000 in the city of monuments, for reasons variously adduced, as: not a theater town, not a Fonda town, snow, rain, Christmas shopping, or—as one producer once said—simply "too dark out." The word was better from Philadelphia, where $20,000 worth of tickets went in two days.

On Wednesday morning my wife arrived, and together we watched the creep-through continue, from two in the afternoon until midnight; detail by detail, the show was being pieced together under Arthur's patient voice, and the new second-act curtain seemed more effective. But the bogdowns, while the actors stood in place for fifteen minutes waiting, made one want to explode, and at one point Fred did, furiously advising Arthur, George, and Pete that it was intolerable planning to treat actors so. Fred was in such a temper that he withdrew to a back corner to silence himself; whether work proceeded any more swiftly thereafter I could not tell, but I was rather pleased to find we had a producer who could shout.

It was not until Thursday afternoon that the lights and sets were ready for our premiere six hours later, and we had our sole dress rehearsal. I thought it not bad. But at its conclusion I was told Hank was abysmally unhappy; Fred sat with him on a bed onstage, sotto voce, for the better part of an hour. I kept apart from this, as did Arthur. Annie on the other hand seemed in untroubled spirits; she, Arthur, my wife, and I ate a convivial dinner out, while Hank stayed behind in his dressing-room.

Shortly before curtain time I went backstage to the performers' make-up cells, kissed Annie on the cheek and Hank on the back of his neck, and then joined the audience. The house was what actors call a barn, of immense capacity, and had been "papered" with passes to fill up the vacuum; the audience—among them a handful of our agents and other theater folk down from New York—was plentiful and buzzy, with many in formal evening garb, including two of the three newspaper critics in town. We delayed the curtain for twenty minutes awaiting the third. Seats had been reserved for Fred, Arthur, and me, but all of us were on our feet in the back aisle, too restive to sit, gathering, separating, regathering; when the house lights at last dimmed, we clutched the back railing and stared at the stage.

The spotlights came up on Hank. In the first two minutes it was evident how withdrawn his performance would be; a friend later described it as done "behind a scrim," this being a gauze curtain used in the theater to suggest underwater effects. Annie played with bravura; we had in rehearsal experimented with toning her down, but with both performers down we simply had no show, so we had recanted; it was another month before we could afford a more truthful performance out of her. The audience performed brilliantly in the first act, which was barely underway when they detonated a guffaw that blew the worry out of my head, I knew they would love all the comedy, and I slipped into my seat beside my wife for the remainder of the show. In the first intermission the lot of us scattered to eavesdrop on them in the lobby, but all I could garner was chitchat about their own selfish concerns. During the second act I was less sure of their enjoyment; here the show dove abruptly from comedy into somberness, leaving them behind it seemed, and I felt that in solving the first act with charm we had shirked preparing them for the body of the play; this was the profile I missed, along with the uncharming violence of my man. The next intermission Fred, Arthur, and I spent together in the manager's office off the lobby, discussing Hank's inaudible—we did in fact receive complaints—performance. Arthur said in gloom, "He makes his point." Our secretary Jessica then slipped in to report that one of the critics liked the show but thought Fonda "had a thankless part," and our faces fell; Fred said, "If that appears in print Hank will want to get out." This criticism so echoed in my head, with a dismay for my own insufficiency as writer, that my eyes took in little of the third act. The curtain calls at its close seemed perfunctory.

I put on a bright countenance, and went backstage to greet the performers. Annie was darting around in a flock of Italians, relatives down from Yonkers, so excited I doubted she heard me. I was admitted to Hank sitting stoop-shouldered at his make-up table; I had been told he was in good spirits, but they seemed to me those of a man who had been pulled out of a dishwater sea.

Afterwards a group of us—Fred and I, our wives, Arthur, our various agents—rode off dull-tongued in a couple of taxis to a private club for theater people, maintained by some wing of the profession to provide a late-hours refuge when other spots were closed; I learned such a club exists in most cities on the road, like an underworld. We were the only celebrants there on this midnight, and not very bacchanalian. Fred ordered drinks, Arthur phoned his extremely pregnant wife, and I tried a few tunes on the piano, but had no heart for it—though I was reassured I could always earn a living *that* way—and we made talk about this and that, skirting the show, until I was asked how I felt. I said very gloomy. Leah and Fred's agent now said Hank would come through with a performance when he had not just an audience but a bigger advance sale, that is, in Philadelphia. I disagreed, I said I thought he was flatly miscast, and I saw no way out of our dilemma: Hank could not play what I wrote, and I could not write what he played. Fred then calmly took over the discussion. While he would not defend the performance he thought we should look to "our own backyard," work was needed on the script along lines which with other casting would have been apparent sooner, and he would talk about these with me the next day. His manner was so firm and undismayed that I saw him with new eyes, a man who could stand against me; a man who could stand against me was one I could lean upon. While we talked, the first of the reviews—by the critic Jessica had quoted—arrived; to our relief, the phrase about "a thankless part" was not quite in print.

We went home to our beds, and it was not until the following day that all three local reviews were in our hands.

11

RICHARD L. COE's review in the *Washington Post* was headed " 'Seesaw' Has Witty Wisdom," and ran thus:

Amusing and touching, "Two on the Seesaw" is a valid two-character play with a basic weakness further magic may dispel. William Gibson's comedy-drama had its premiere (genuine brand!) last night at the Shubert with Henry Fonda and Anne Bancroft, assisted by two telephones, as the cast.

Miss Bancroft has the more ingratiating assignment, a slightly coarse girl of the Bronx who fancies herself as a modern dancer ("Whaddya mean, who's Jose?") and finds herself mixed up with the immature libido of a Nebraska lawyer trying to shake off a wife who has tried to do too much for him.

Their brash, but hesitant courtship forms the first act, merry listening for it is most adroitly played. Gibson's view of the dancer will strike those who've been inside the dance-world as straight from life and Miss Bancroft embarks on her wise, cynical homilies with contagious relish.

Fonda's role is infinitely more difficult and he plays it with a fine actor's intelligence of its pitfalls. For, as Gibson reveals him, Jerry Ryan is a fellow who can try our patience. We are not always willing to accept his idea that a well-set-up Nebraska lawyer will live in a sleazy $21 a month New

York flat with little contacts in his profession and virtually no friends. One questions.

Is this fair to the story? No, for what is ailing Jerry is a more serious matter to which Gittel wishes to turn our thoughts. He is one of those fellows who short change those whom he says he loves. He has given so much of himself to his wife, but not, evidently, all. The same pattern follows with the dancer he met so casually.

Thus, Fonda must capture us on two levels, and it seems almost asking the unnecessary. However, he plays the fellow with ingenious skill, shifts of command and nice mixtures of dry humor and appeal. With some cutting and further experience in their second act scenes I've little doubt that one will not have time to think of these things.

But if plot and character are of import to plays, so is dialogue and here Gibson does extremely well by players and audience. For the most part his lines are amusingly drawn from character and the girl is a refreshingly observed individual. Her milieu is, of course, more vivid than the man's and Gibson has caught it colorfully.

Fred Coe's production hasn't spared the bankroll. There are adroitly varied views of two rooms by George Jenkins, a deft method of sharpening our vision. Arthur Penn's direction, at its best for the lighter moments, is aware of the serious ones which still smack of self-consciousness.

For all these reservations, "Two for the Seesaw" is an enjoyable, usually interesting evening. It will, I think, improve immeasurably with a few performances and some incisive cutting.

Jay Carmody's review in the *Evening Star* was headed "Fonda a Busy Star in Shubert's Play":

William Gibson tries something of a tour de force in writing "Two for the Seesaw," which opened a 17-day engagement at the Shubert Theatre last night.

He has written a two-character play, the performers Henry Fonda and Anne Bancroft, which has a lot to say of how much lostness and loneliness can be found in a mere pair of lives. The quantity of these two qualities may seem a little overpowering to more rugged bumblers like the rest of us, as indeed it did even to Miss Bancroft and Mr. Fonda last night.

In both cases, this may be explained by the fact that the performance was the first anywhere for "Two for the Seesaw." If this turns out to be true, it should take some of the tedium out of Mr. Gibson's play for audiences, without adversely affecting what it has to reveal of human torment.

Like "The Fourposter," the last two-character play, the new one also centers around a bed, but a less respectable one. The latter not only lacks the sanction of marriage but also is occupied by creatures of less emotional range who are inclined to stammer instead of speaking out.

There is nothing wrong with this, at least as play theme. Yet the sight of miserably trapped creatures on a stage can give theatregoers an uncomfortable feeling the same fate is overtaking them. Unfortunately, this is true of the Shubert's play in spite of the valiance of its two busy stars.

Mr. Fonda and Miss Bancroft are a dramatically assorted pair in the situation Mr. Gibson has chosen to explore.

He is a refugee from a cloying marriage and a legal career in Omaha who has fled to New York for escape. He holes up in a furnished room in a seedy part of town, lost to the world until he meets a girl who divides her time between making stage costumes and dreaming of being a great modern dancer.

This head-on crash of their mutual loneliness is productive of much that is amusing, such unlikely types they are, and more that is desperately hungry. The intimations of the play are that Mr. Gibson has given this sort of thing a lot of study. Being a good student, his report on it is both hu-

morously and agonizingly detailed in the mercurial moodiness of the principals.

Neither of these quite know what the other wants. Having far the better mind, Fonda's man is convinced that it is high time he learned to be a giver instead of a mere taker. This decent intention, with its therapeutic promise, is unwittingly frustrated by the girl.

In the vernacular, she is a good-hearted slob, pretty and shamelessly generous. She does not know how NOT to give and until she is laid low by a hemorrhaging ulcer, Fonda makes zero headway in showing he, too, can be generous.

The effect is to keep the play rather longer on dead-center than is easily bearable for a mere outsider.

Working in a remarkably flexible mechanism designed by George Jenkins, Mr. Fonda and Miss Bancroft are an extraordinarily tireless pair.

As the articulate one, for all his befuddlement, it is the former's responsibility to make Miss Bancroft see how complex life can be. His, then, is the predicament of an adult trying to make a child understand what the latter already sees more clearly than anyone else.

With a play partner as vivacious as Miss Bancroft, this effort of Fonda's comes off as both funny and touching. Her Jewish directness, her habit of calling a spade something more blood-curdling, and her sense of the relationship's ultimate futility are affecting. But no more than Fonda's efforts do they carry the conviction that their common plight is as interesting as Mr. Gibson is arguing.

It is possible that Director Arthur Penn will find the key to the importance of what "Two for the Seesaw" is trying to say. Two-character plays can be quite a special problem in this respect as "The Fourposter" certainly proved in its shakedown days.

In the end, they must have more than the mere novelty of two characters and a set as strikingly versatile as the tan-

dem bedrooms Mr. Jenkins has designed for "Two for the Seesaw."

Tom Donnelly's review in the *Washington Daily News* was headed "A Boy, a Girl, a Telephone":

The heroine of William Gibson's "Two for the Seesaw" (at the Shubert) is a riotously colorful young woman named Gittel Mosca. Gittel is a native of the Bronx, and she speaks the wonderful language of that region fluently. She says, to a friend on the phone: "So what do you think I'm crazy? I take him home to meet Mom and he'll leave New York in a balloon!"

The man in question is Jerry Ryan, a lawyer from Omaha, Neb. When Jerry meets Gittel he is in a state of sour rebellion. His wife has left him for another man, he still loves her, he is ashamed that he has accepted uncounted favors from his father-in-law, he is alone in New York where he is not of course able to practice, and he is so fed up with things that he crashes a fist thru a window in his dingy flat.

Gittel brings tumult and carnival into his life. She is pretty, resolutely cheerful, profane, fantastically generous with her possessions and with her person, and afflicted with ulcers. Jerry wants to turn their first date into an all-night affair. Gittel says she is not that kind of a girl. Jerry says it is his birthday. Gittel reconsiders: after all, if it's the poor guy's birthday. . . . But Jerry also reconsiders. He does not want to play on Gittel's sympathy; he has had enough of "asking for hand-outs."

And so it goes. They quarrel, they make love, they try to understand one another. Because of him, she acquires a certain strength. Because of her, he acquires a certain softness. For approximately half the distance Mr. Gibson's composition for two characters and a telephone is an attractive bittersweet comedy, with Gittel shining thru as a kind of Fanny Brice variation on the girl in "The Voice of the Turtle."

Later on, "Two for the Seesaw" grows increasingly solemn. Jerry finds himself torn between two ailing women: Gittel's ulcer is acting up something fierce, and his offstage wife, who doesn't seem to want that divorce any more, is having a nervous breakdown. Mr. Gibson has perhaps introduced too many notes from the Bette Davis Symphony. And surely Gittel and Jerry should not take to discussing their problems with such tedious intensity: you'd think they had the hash of the Western world to settle.

Even in its present inflated state "Two for the Seesaw" is an acceptable diversion. Henry Fonda is, as always, a most ingratiating performer, and he succeeds in putting a pleasant gloss on Jerry, a fellow Ann Landers would dismiss at a glance as an unsavory specimen. Anne Bancroft somewhat overplays Gittel in the preliminaries, but she soon settles down to giving a performance that is altogether delightful.

12

I awoke early, and heavy in heart even prior to reading these reviews, which then lay upon me all day like a blanket of earth; the occasional flowers in them were unseeable from below.

My wife and I spent the first half of the day in our room chewing over the premiere with three visitors in succession, Leah, Arthur, and a friend in show business. The consensus on Annie's performance was ardent: Leah called her "a magnificent instrument," and when I asked whether in my friend's opinion she could play the lead in *The Miracle Worker*—Arthur and I had been casting this mentally for several weeks—he said, "I think she can play anything." The consensus on the total show was less ardent, and that on the script awaited my afternoon session with Fred and Arthur.

On our way to this my wife and I downstairs stepped into a taxi that Annie stepped out of; Annie said later my face made her "feel like crying," an astonishing observation to a man who thought of himself as a poker-face; I was to lose more than one such illusion. At the theater we collected Arthur and Fred, who were working on things that had gone awry in performance—scene changes had taken minutes instead of seconds, a clothes rod had refused to fall on cue, the oven in which the girl was cooking a sumptuous repast had turned out to be empty—and we repaired to the ladies' lounge for our conference.

Their topic was, as always, my man. I accepted Fred's talking percentage that our problem was fifty per cent in the writing of him, provided we reserved the other fifty per cent, the acting and direction, for a separate session. Arthur and Fred then discoursed at me for an hour, with irresistible intelligence, while I felt my face setting like cement, its expression no doubt saying get through if you can, but listening. Stripped of complexities, their position was that the character—Arthur later added, as played—could not hold the audience unless it were made more appealing, that is, more giving to the girl. I was readier to concede this than they knew, but Arthur was intent on reaching me and labeled my man a "liar" and a "cheat," documenting it in detail, with a relentlessness I felt he omitted in his handling of Hank. What was under attack was a major dimension of the character as I had conceived him, exploiting and self-concerned, which in the course of the guilt-bound affair onstage he was himself to perceive and redeem; it was at the root of his marital wilt, and having lived it through with the girl, he was to return for a better try at the marriage; it thus constituted one mainspring of the play, and the curve of the character throughout. On the record, I had to grant my failure to write this curve persuasively. The failure to act and direct for the curve had compounded mine; we had yet to see it embodied onstage, I was devoid of belief that we ever would, and I had no evidence to argue in the teeth of the reviews that any audience would find it interesting. When I reappeared from behind my facial cement, it was to specify and explore ways I saw to make the man not more individual—less, I thought, in forfeiting this inner dynamic—but morally palatable.

I thus beheaded the concept, and with it a serious developmental aspect of the drama, with no conviction that it was after a fair trial by its peers; it was in fact the lack thereof that compelled the verdict, and I accepted Arthur's man as a workable substitute. I no more wanted a tedious flop than he did, and we turned the face of the script toward romance. I could console myself of course that my primary love in the play was the girl, who in both the writing and the performance was undamageable. But in this moment I crossed a line between two worlds of writing: henceforth material was to be shaped less by what I had to say than by what the audience would listen to. I would in time experience this as demoralizing to my self-respect and belief in the play; at present, there was much rewriting to be done, and with this call to action I revived, again a willing accomplice. The rewriting spanned all of the second act, which we examined for another hour, so it was dinner-time before we gave the lounge back to the ladies.

The performance that evening seemed somewhat better, and was greeted by warmer, though still tepid, curtain calls. Halfway through it I put my wife in a taxi, and it bore her off toward the night train, Massachusetts, and our boys. At midnight Fred, Arthur, and I at my request reconvened in Arthur's room for my licks, which took until two-thirty.

I said in part: I would proceed with all energy to the rewriting we had outlined; but the immutable fact was that God had written Gittel in heaven and I had written Jerry in Stockbridge, doing all that mortal man could (Fred said calmly, "You will do more"); no further rewriting would make a significant difference if the performance remained as it was; what was imperative onstage was not a "sympathetic" color, but a dramatic one, of any hue, which we lacked because we had not reached and opened Hank; and someone—if not Arthur, then I—must work with him around the clock, day after day, to achieve that color by any technique, even imitative. Arthur said he was not optimistic about the results. I said failing this I had to ask Fred whether a cryptic remark of his the night before had implied the possibility of Hank's leaving, Fred said it had, and I said I would like that possibility explored. I said on the other hand: of all our traps, Hank was in the most agonizing; his accepting the part now seemed misjudgment of the play (Fred said Hank was "doing the longest double take of his life") and his own decision; nevertheless he was also being used, and we had a human responsibility to him which we had not fulfilled. Arthur said it was difficult to undertake without hope, and I said but that was the ultimate generosity, it was how I would be rewriting, and I floated upstairs to bed on a benign confluence of brotherly and self-love.

Neither survived my next view of the show. I spent Saturday morning in my room, beginning the second-act revision, took a taxi to the theater to catch the matinee, and perceived my work was doomed. The performance was limp, paceless, even the scene where the man blew in like a windstorm was now becalmed. I told Arthur it was getting worse instead of better, and took a taxi back to the hotel, where I wrote and mailed my agent a letter—she had returned to New York—asking her to look into Fritz Weaver's present commitments; the play he was in had flopped. I then continued the rewrite.

Arthur and Fred had a post-matinee session with Hank, and that evening the performance showed a qualitative step-up in energy. My letter about Weaver seemed a superfluity.

I rewrote throughout the next two days. Fred and Arthur stopped in before dinner on Sunday to listen to the tenor of my second-act opening—now appreciably lighter and more affirmative—and approved it, but the gloom of their afternoon rehearsal was upon them; Hank had been down again. They invited me along to a nearby restaurant, to eat with the cast and Fred's wife. During dinner Hank told us of his difficulties with the director and unreal dialogue of a recent movie, and I remembered that at lunch in New York he had told us of his difficulties with another playwright's unreal dialogue in another movie; we were in a business like a grab bag, where no one got what he wanted. Afterwards I stood on a sidewalk and pathetically watched the five of them ride off in a taxi to a hilarious movie (which happily turned out to be even more pathetic), then went for a long walk past the dark national headquarters of some odd organizations, and returned to my cell to rewrite until one in the morning. I was at it again bright and early and all the next day, while rehearsal was in progress in the outside world, and towards evening I delivered the scene to Jessica. She skipped the performance that night—usually she sat in the back row with a clip-board winking under a tiny light, and jotted down Arthur's and anyone else's critical notes—and typed in her room, on a chair and two phone books, rushing copies for the producer, director, cast, stand-bys, and stage managers. I rode off to the theater in good spirits after my bout of work.

This time they failed to survive the first act. In the intermission I asked Arthur why the performance was again so limp; he said there had been an agreement to let Hank play it that night as he thought proper. I walked out of the theater. I continued to walk until I was back at the hotel, a mile or two of my head accumulating steam pressure like a boiler, the calmest of the visions in it being to reclaim the new scene, board a train with it, and disappear out of everyone's hand. Instead I went to Jessica's room, found her still on the two phone books, drank some of her brandy, and phoned Leah at home in New York; I told her I had to be posted on Weaver. I blew off some steam in talk with Jessica, accepted her invitation to cocoa later with her and Annie, then went to my own room and blew off some more in an epistle to Arthur. I left it for him downstairs at the desk. In it I said that I was pursuing an inquiry into Weaver's commitments; that I must see Arthur work up Kevin—with whose acting I was still unacquainted—in one scene by the end of the week; that I was disappointed to find, instead of our agreement to work Hank, an agreement to let him play it his own way; and that I thought he must be "fought to the ground" to see whether he was in or out of the show, since at present he was neither. In my room again I settled on the bed with the rewriting, but I was blind to it. About eleven-thirty Arthur phoned from downstairs, and came up to discuss the wrath in my note. He said I had misconstrued his agreement with Hank, which was temporary and explorative; I asked was he afraid of Hank or afraid of losing him for the show, Arthur said the latter, and I said I was willing to lose him if Arthur was; he consented to our putting it so to Fred that night. Fred walked in, and I put it. Fred said he had gone into the matter with Joey, whose opinion was that it meant forfeiting our advance sale, raising another $80,000, and starting over from scratch: in a word, disaster. I said that seemed to be that. Relieved of this decision, and not unrelieved to be, I courteously abandoned Arthur and Fred in my room and went down to join the lower echelons; among Kevin, Gaby, Jessica, and Annie, I refreshed myself with the pleasures of irresponsible malcontentism, and went to bed at four a.m. purged of my poisons.

I was electing Kevin as my conscience: he disapproved of all the changes I had made in the man's lines, and in the wee hours I had been explaining them—to my satisfaction, if not his—as surrenders made not to commerce but to the art of the theater, wherein a diversity of talents must lop and trim to converge in a single onstage statement. The next day I received a letter from a playwright who had seen our New York run-through and Washington premiere, and offered criticisms which Arthur had relayed to me; I flinched at the sight of the plump envelope. But when I opened it, I read paragraph after paragraph I might have mailed to myself:

At this moment you probably have a very real headache, an upset stomach, you can't fall asleep and you can't stay awake, you hate everybody in the world, particularly Arthur and Fred and Henry Fonda and Anne Bancroft and Margaret and your goddam kids and the whole theatregoing public. . . . I have not too long ago gone through exactly what you are going through. . . . I know the frustrating agony of writing one play and seeing a completely different one on the stage, and I know that it particularly hurts when you write the play not out of a "let me see, what would be a good idea for a play" kind of thing, but out of a real and personal and important experience that you have gone through. In my case, as in yours, I wrote what I thought to be a pretty serious play, but by the time we got through with it (or by the time Philadelphia got through with us) the entire concept was changed. . . . I was faced with these facts: given the star, the cast, the director, the set, I could never get anything remotely close to what I wanted. I could refuse to make the compromise, have a flop play, and write articles saying how my beautiful work was ruined and all of that; or I could take the materials at hand and see how I could use them, forgetting what I had started out to do, and concentrating on what I could do from that moment on. . . . The hard facts seem to be that everybody in the theatre does make compromises and the theatre is none the worse for it, because the truth is nobody knows what our private hopes and anguishes are. You liked my play very much, I'm told, and since I very much respect your opinion I can only gather that my reactions to the play are not reliable because all I could see was my own compromise. . . . We made our compromises long before rehearsals started, and once having made them we are committed to them, and obligated to serve them instead of denying and fighting them. Nobody will care about the private plays we had in our heads, if what they see on the

> *stage is good and complete and holds together as a whole and separate entity. If what they see is two separate plays, the one we wrote and the one being acted, very few people will be able to say it's not the playwright's fault. What they say is, the wonderful actors did the best with what they had to work with. . . . In the final analysis it is the playwright's responsibility to be the most mature one in the crisis.*

And later that week my wife wrote, about a TV show by still another playwright who had written a stage play the season before:

> *It was a very honest piece about a group of people getting a show to Broadway. . . . The story seems always to be the same, point for point. The writer says in agony, "That's not my play they're acting at all." The director says to the writer, "You must realize even if it hurts that show business involves a lot of people." The writer to the director, "Why is it that you, my good friend, seem to be my enemy when you are directing a play of mine?" And so on. It was almost comic.*

Obviously my experience was in no way notable, a fact which alone justified noting it down in exhaustive detail.

It was agreed among the brain trust, as I laughingly called Fred, Arthur, and me, that since witnessing the art of the theater so diminished my zest in contributing to it I should stay in my room during performances. Accordingly I skipped the next three. These were my first absences, but of the three-dozen shows to come I missed two dozen, and the bulk of rehearsals as well. I spent most of these days and nights repointing pencils in a portable sharpener provided by Jessica.

I now moved on to another scene, but I was not so easily free of the one I had already lightened: on Tuesday Fred came to me from rehearsal with a half-dozen passages of Hank's to be rerewritten for more color, and on Wednesday Arthur came from the matinee to ask for still another ending to the scene, closer to the somberness of the original. This was really responsible; it seemed ironic that Arthur was now protecting my script against me. But I had crossed the line: I was no longer in my inner world of writing, where the logic was that of a lifetime, but in the outer world of show business, where the logic was only that of this production, evolved to meet the emergencies of our situation; Fred said I was "buying things too easily," but if I could not have my logic, it was a matter of relative indifference to me which of the other logics we followed. I rewrote the rewrites, and on Thursday completed for the third time a later scene.

My confinement was varied by more social moments: Fred would stop in with a gift of pipe tobacco, Jessica and I would exchange coffee visits, Annie would look in after the show, Arthur would revive me with a drink in his room, and I had dinner each night with some or all of them in the cozy dining-room downstairs. Hank and his wife were in the hotel, but I rarely saw them. Leah meanwhile phoned to inform me that Weaver had no commitments prior to doing Hamlet, a better part, at the American Shakespeare Festival next summer. Though the news was now unusable, I could not believe my own blow-up was without directorial reverberations in the rehearsals in outer space: at a cocoa party in Jessica's room after the Tuesday performance I heard Hank had played it high, and I took as proof Arthur's jokes, which were very fast and funny. The next performance—I had characterized the work with actors in *The Miracle Worker* as doing snow sculpture at noonday under an August sun—was reported as low again. The heat was a *Variety* review hailing Annie but critical of me and Hank, which I was told occasioned a scene, Hank saying to Fred maybe we should get rid of him, and Fred saying or maybe he should get rid of us, which was it? Thirty-nine angels danced on the point of this pin, since if we separated from Hank we were liable for his contract, but if he separated from us we were not.

Yet our plight was gay, weighed on the scales of the profession; the two other shows in town had opened before us to reviews which made ours read like hosannas. One of them, badly in need of work, was down to its last dollar, could not afford to stay out another day, and was going into New York to certain doom. Visitors from our company to theirs reported back that the despondency could be sliced with a knife; it was not glory that concerned them, but a foundering business, and daily bread and butter in the months ahead for the actors, writers, director, crew, and the families at their heels. As for the other show, its brain trust was resident in our hotel, waking Arthur with all-night conferences in the room next to his, the director's voice exploding in the majestic ring of English, "I'll tell you what she's gaht, she's gaht the fuhkeeng stah qualitih!" I would see these five, all in dark suits, at their damasked table in the dining-room, eating in funereal silence; the producer was pointed out to me with some awe as a man who had produced fourteen flops in a row. Then they disappeared, and also were buried in New York. We were in competition with these two shows, the business they lost we gained, but we were made kin by a nimbus in common, of esprit de corps, morituri te salutamus, oi veh.

Thursday morning Arthur began—and finished, as events proved—understudy rehearsals, to give me a look at Kevin by the weekend. At the dinner table that evening with the Coes and him, I blew off at Arthur again over a touchy point, largely personal; he flushed and said I seemed "swift to anger" with him. It was true, I was in a state of chronic vexation under my skin, with him and with Hank, singly and together. In this smoulder I proceeded to outline my view of the rewriting to come in another scene, as against Fred's and Arthur's view. In the middle of it I said to Arthur's downbent face, "Are you hearing me?" and he said tersely, "Somewhat." Fred thought we had enough worries without the playwright and director now being embattled; still angry I said that was no serious problem betwixt brothers, still terse Arthur agreed, and leaving the scene unresolved and my meal uneaten, I took off for the theater alone.

Pending an agreement among us on the scene I had no writing to do, and I wanted to watch a performance from the bridge backstage. This was not the show I had written, but the reality behind it: below me a small army—twenty stagehands, dressers, stage managers, prop men, electricians—swarmed around Annie and Hank in a fever of preparations; on warning, they melted into the ground, and the curtain rose on the two actors alone in their stage-set world with their fictional chatter; at the end of the scene the blackout curtain fell, worklights glared on the twin shells of rooms swinging in counterpoint off and on and roundabout like carousels, repopulated in motion by a tide of anonymous workers who obscured our stars now in the hands of their dressers making frantic ten-second changes of costume; on warning, everything real again vanished, and only the illusion remained in the rise of the curtain. To create this illusion we were breaking each other's hearts, digestive systems, and brainpans. Midway in the show Fred joined me on the bridge, and aware of my desolateness, kept me company till the end; I was grateful, and was coming to respect his quiet (when not shouting) sense more each day.

I stopped in on Arthur's room after midnight to make my peace with him. He had been through a difficult day himself, with Annie somehow obstructive over the new material—while I was there she phoned him to make *her* peace—and I knew that he was also on edge awaiting at any hour a summons from New York to another drama, of different illusions and staggering reality. Not six hours later I was awakened by my phone: it was Arthur, to say his wife's labor had begun, he was off for home, and rehearsals would be in Fred's and my hands until his return.

With this reassignment to rehearsals, I began—it was our fortieth day—upon five days which brought my own involvement with the production to a climax.

Friday morning in my room Fred and I resumed discussion of the unrewritten scene, and in the afternoon convened with the company on the tarpaulin again. It was now laid on the floor of an upstairs dining-hall in a cafeteria; rehearsals had been held here for the past week of my incarceration, since using the theater would entail certain extravagances, such as a crew of union electricians to turn on the light switch, which we could not yet afford. Here Fred and I somewhat shyly interfered with each other in co-directing a placid rehearsal, with Fred allowing me the lion's share. What we worked upon was the rewritten scene which opened the second act; new material like this was memorized by the actors after midnight, rehearsed in one assimilable chunk the next day, and put into the show the same evening. (Such insertions made the play a bit enigmatic for our Washington audiences, most of whom saw a second act that traveled simultaneously toward opposite destinations.) Dealing directly with Hank I felt, illusorily or not, the beginnings of communication. He was discovering that the stage business written into the text—stage folk ignore the playwright's instructions on principle—was helpful; and he was helpful himself with the staging, acting out for Annie's use a pantomimic travesty of modern-dance movement which had until now failed to evoke the laugh we intended it to.

In performance that evening the laugh came. The show otherwise, after the first act, was slow and dissipated; it was exasperating for all of us to work with material we knew was scheduled for junking, but I urged Fred to exhort the actors to pace, by which I meant plain celerity. I joined Hank and the Coes in a midnight supper, though I had little stomach for either food or social life.

No word from Arthur awaited us at the hotel that night, and the silence continued throughout the next day; I commenced to worry about obstetric difficulties. I skipped the Saturday matinee, and worked all day rewriting. Fred stopped in to say the matinee had been good, and faster by a couple of minutes. News suddenly arrived that Arthur had been the father of a sturdy boy for almost twenty-four hours; the message had been pocketed backstage by a stagehand who if unasked might have carried it with him to the grave.

Arthur arrived on its heels, shining. I had two decisions on *The Miracle Worker* ready to submit to him. I had been offered a co-production deal on it, whereby at no cost Arthur and I would each own a third of the producer's half; in money terms this was dazzling, but I had been withholding my assent until I saw how a producer should look in action. I now knew. Arthur's taste and talent I wore as familiarly as a shoe of my own, but a comfort to me I had not foreseen was the affirmative knowledgeableness with which Fred was challenging the work in all departments, script, staging, acting, lighting, what not; Arthur's intelligence was fleet, Fred's was earthy, and both acted as a corrective upon mine, which I chafed under but needed. This two-faced reaction was a confusion in me; I did not yet understand how each could be valid. But I said that to be in our present predicament without such a man was a fearful thought, and that if Arthur had no objections I was prepared to offer *The Miracle Worker* to him, with—the second decision—Annie in the lead. Arthur without a blink at his third of a vanishing gold mine said fine. We then took a taxi to the theater, picked up a friend of mine and his fiancée, gulped down some chili across the street, and walked back in to view the performance.

I settled behind my friend, and at the end of the first act, supposedly our good one, he delivered over his shoulder such a devastating criticism of the man as acted that the floor of my mind soundlessly cracked. After the curtain calls I told Fred backstage that if he wanted *The Miracle Worker* it was his; he touched my sleeve and said, "Bless you." I came back alone to the hotel and in my room sat with the rewriting, but the crack widened, and the variety of lava I had compressed for forty-one days flowed out. I tried to write, paced, to read, paced, to listen to music, paced, and at three o'clock switched off the lamp and went to bed; at four o'clock I switched it on again, paced, wrote a letter home outlining three alternative paths for the production, each hopeless, paced, and understood what a stroke of literary genius the cliché to want to jump out of one's skin was; and at five-thirty I did something almost unprecedented in my life, turned to a fellow human because my own society was intolerable. I telephoned Jessica. Her voice swam gallantly up out of sleep to invite me down for brandy coffee, over which we sat talking about the show and ourselves until the venetian blind was gray with eight o'clock light. I then went upstairs to bed, and slept for two and a half hours.

At Sunday brunch with Annie and Jessica—my stomach was still so full of elephants' feet that after introducing one pancake I abandoned the project—I offered Annie the lead in *The Miracle Worker.* (She said wide-eyed and worried, "You think I'm right for it?") Fred had asked that I continue to come to rehearsals, which now moved onstage regardless of expense. That day Arthur restaged a third-act scene, and we read through the rewritten scene which closed the second act; in both scenes, now having my foot like a salesman in the directorial door, I hawked my wares straight to the actors. After rehearsal all of us gathered for drinks in Hank's suite at the hotel, then ate dinner in a Chinese restaurant nearby, where I picked at my food, and we walked back in twos and threes to work in the suite. This was my initiation into Hank's rooms, a fact not unsymbolic of rapprochement; and Fred later told me that on the walk back Hank had expressed some appreciation of me, which encouraged me on toward the brink I was approaching. Our intent to read further in the new scene was derailed by a preliminary word between Hank and me on performing the first act, which burgeoned to usurp the entire evening. This discussion was mutually attentive, vigorous but without acrimony. In response to another sketching by me of the absent profile, Hank said in effect it was a beautiful play and he wished I had written it for him to act, but if I thought Jerry's internal complexes could dominate a stageful of Gittel's external charms I was "living in a dream world." Fred concurred, saying I had "put Hamlet and a clown on the same stage" and the audience's eye inevitably went to the clown. Arthur contributed a new solution to the material in question, which entailed rewriting the man in it to make what was internal more explicit and what was characterologically weak more acceptable. It was after midnight when I went to bed in some bafflement at how my efforts to rally the collective arts of the theater to my aid seemed always to end in my rallying to theirs.

But sometime in the dark thereafter my phone woke me. It was Annie's voice, asking could she alter a word in one line, I said all right, she said her head was swimming with the play, I said ahuh, and I went back to sleep. In the morning I was brewing coffee when she came in to conclude the conversation: she had worked all night, on not her role but the man's, to justify her own opinion that Hamlet could dominate the clown by intensity rather than competitive charms. She now took my room as the stage and somberly acted the man for me. I sat with my coffee and watched her, both amused and impressed; except for her skirt it would have been excellent casting. When we were in a taxi with Arthur en route to the theater, I helpfully suggested that we have her create the man's role for him, which he could then work into the show; Arthur's face froze, and he said he thought such aid unusable. The affront was mostly unwitting.

In this mood—what was quite unwitting was that out of it that day would pounce my jack-in-the-box effort to change everything—I watched rehearsal commence with the second-act finale on its feet. It had been rewritten three times, to Fred's and Arthur's specifications, and been read through on two preceding days. Hank now found so many unactable transitions in it that I sat on the stage floor with paper and pencil and told him to dictate to me what he would prefer to say at every such point, I would deliver his own content to him the next day; and working through the scene again from the beginning, with my pencil busy and ear wincing, we followed this procedure. There was a stinger in its tail, but I myself had no prescience of it until we arrived at a crucial moment in the act. The girl here in a passionate speech indicted the man as a cheat in human commitments; the man, after what I had marked as a "shaken" silence, admitted its truth. This silence as always was elided, and suddenly the jack-in-the-box said in my voice, "I'd like that moment made visible." Hank asked what moment, I said the wordless one in which the man reacted, Hank said how could that be made visible, and I said it was not in my province, had nothing to do with writing, was a problem exclusively in acting and direction, and I wanted him and Arthur to make it visible. I took to a chair onstage and waited. This dialogueless moment now became a battlefield for an hour, in which Arthur stood silently thinking, and I said, "Hank, I've met you halfway from the start and you haven't met me ten per cent," and Hank said, "Well, Bill, it's hard," and I moved over to the proscenium arch to wait it out in ostensible calm, my limbs trembling although I was on the most solid ground of my life, and Fred mounted the stage to back me, saying what I was asking for was "part of every actor's kit," and upon the ensuing debate, which in language and lunguage violated parliamentary rules, I here pull down the shade. Ultimately the moment was solved by Arthur and Hank deciding upon a turn upstage.

On my way out of rehearsal Fred, in the seats with his agent, stopped my arm and asked me to do him a favor, speak with Hank, have a drink with him, invite him to dinner. I said I would speak with him, and climbing back onstage I intercepted Hank on the stairs to his dressing-room. I had no idea what I was to say, and said so; Hank said he did not know what to say either, except he wished he could explain to me how something could read well for literary reasons and still be unplayable; I said it was not unplayable, and he said, "Then I'm miscast." It was a logical conclusion, and he had articulated it on several occasions, when none of us would give him a straight answer. Nor did I; I said if he played the man I had written he could have the triumph of his life, and I would be actively involved in every moment of rehearsals from now on.

Fred and his agent met for dinner with Arthur and me, but the group did not survive the cocktails; a cryptic dispute sprang up between Fred and the agent concerning the work, and Fred in a spume about "hypocrisy" walked irately out of the restaurant. The three of us chewed our way brightly through a rubbery dinner. The agent said her point was that some concessions should be made to Hank, and Arthur said the afternoon was the culmination of six weeks of concessions she was ignorant of. I said I thought we had that day finally separated the issues: hitherto we had been splitting the difference, in a fifty-fifty compromise on each point regardless of its merits, but henceforth when Hank was right I would yield one hundred per cent on rewriting and when he was wrong I would demand one hundred per cent on acting.

It was a new day—the show that night was neither bad nor good—before I commenced on my half of this program. I devoted the morning to polishing the speeches I had taken out of Hank's mouth. I then made another attempt to smuggle some food past the elephants' feet, without success, after which I took the speeches and feet with me in a taxi to rehearsal. It was already in progress, and I stood onstage to one side, in wait for the other half of the program. I had made up my mind that I would in this rehearsal give Hank the straight answer—that I agreed he was miscast—and see where we went from there.

I had never felt so strangely weak in my life. I had no inner choice except the fight to the ground I had recommended to Arthur, to determine whether Hank was in or out of the show, and my bones wavered at the prospect; I had only a glimmer of which alternative it would end in, I was on the brink either of the disaster Joey saw or of an uncovered bedrock for work without evasions; and I was about to gamble the production on a megalomanic image of myself in a state of wrestling blood-brotherhood with a man no one had come close to. I had reached much more inaccessible souls in my drama group at the psychiatric institution, but never by any means other than straight answers; and in one of my various views we had failed an honest man by supplying a paste of cosmetic concessions in lieu of a commitment in the bowels of truth. On the other heart, I had murder in me. I suspected this was the indispensable energy in any such cementing, but at this rehearsal I felt drained of all energies, my inner organs in anarchy, my spleen in my mouth, my intestines clogging my windpipe, my brains in my feet wishing to run; my legs did their utmost, they held me erect. I was not onstage five minutes when Fred beckoned me down to the seats, to ask for a session with me.

I followed him to the manager's office off the lobby, where Fred sat in a desk chair and I collapsed at full length on a divan. I had no foreknowledge of what was in Fred's mind, but perhaps he smelt what was in mine, because he asked me to go back to the hotel. He could not see how else I would find time for the rewriting, and tabulated all the spots in the man's role he thought still needed it; this was the vulnerable heel in my otherwise righteous, though supine, position; it was this one doubt, present from our beginnings on, that made the undercutting of my shaky intent ineludible. Fred meanwhile said he was "not yet panicky" but was closer to it, and the sight of me in dissolution on the divan did not help. I waved my hand luxuriously and told him not to worry about me, my energies were inexhaustible, meanwhile wondering baffledly how I was to get to my feet. I said we had made a deal after the premiere, quoted his words that when I rewrote the second act I would "have a perfect right to holler," and said now I was claiming that right; he said but I had not delivered my half of the deal, one scene was not finished; I said but only because he had called me away from it back to rehearsals, nevertheless that was irrelevant, I had two sizeable questions to ask. I said I knew the answer to the first: who would come to terms with Hank if I did not? nobody. The second was whether Fred was convinced, and could tell me without qualification, that my major contribution to the show should now be in my capacity solely as writer. Fred said, "Absolutely." I said that was good enough for me, my inner organs commenced to slide back into their usual localities, and I successfully stood up. I had only one condition, which Fred acceded to: I was not to hear a word henceforth about any of their difficulties with Hank.

I went back onstage and told Hank I was reneging on my promise, my availability at rehearsals was to become zero because Fred had asked me to retire to write; Hank said he understood. Rehearsal was in abeyance, with Annie on the bed paralyzed by gynecic cramps—it was exactly twenty-eight days to our New York opening, if we needed something to worry about—and Arthur excused her for the afternoon. I helped her back to the hotel in a taxi and up to her bed, ordered a pot of tea from room service, drew her blinds, and went to my own room to sit and ponder. I was in one piece again, and I digested the events of the week, like a repulsive sundae, so many scoops of rage, sprinkled with loss of appetite, nutty with sleeplessness, and topped that day by a generous goo of physiological chaos.

I knew I had experienced for the first time in my life an attack of clinical anxiety. I was familiar with the symptomatology, I was married to a psychoanalyst, I had myself worked with patients, I had even written a novel about a psychiatric hospital which was in use by teachers as a textbook, but my religion was will: anxiety to me was hearsay. I had outwitted it for almost half a century by two stratagems. One was of the mind, in the deflection of my painful matter away from real faces and into literary fantasy and forms; this avenue was now road-blocked at both ends, by the unfleeable faces of my collaborators and the need for a commodity type of writing much more concerned with the audience's pains than with mine. The other was of the body, in the invention of a duodenal ulcer—which I had generously shared with my character Gittel —as a garbage pail for unwanted feelings; under the present onslaught of tension and dietary abuse it had disobeyed all the doctors, and was as intact and healthy as apple skin. The feelings it denied admission to had broken through another wall entirely. I had caught a glimpse of a pit in which the acids of the mind could nullify the body and dissolve the concepts of free will, choice, action, into a smoke of inane verbiage.

I was dazzled. I had come upon a deep treasure, and knew it. I had thought of my play as altering the lives of all its participants in unsuspected fashion; but in return they had altered mine, I felt united at last to the body of human mishap, and nothing I valued in the world—family, work, health —would be unleavened by it. It was of much less consequence now whether the play died or not: I was alive in a new way.

ACT THREE

December 1957 – *July* 1958

With this aborted showdown my sense of participancy in the production reached its highwater mark, and commenced to fall back upon itself. The six weeks of our three-way tug-of-war—among actor, director, playwright—culminated in an uneasy standstill, which fulfilled no one; but out of it work as usual was possible. I saw that in the rewriting I had my own rope to hang on, in both senses. Fred said that successful theater consisted of "making the right compromise at the right time," and events proved his calling me off to have been sage captaincy; Arthur later said he could see in my move only "the end of the production," at least as we knew it; and I was too grateful at the lifting of my own inner disunity to insist. The heart of the matter thus was never cracked, eruptions too repetitive to chronicle here pocked the next month of rehearsals, and in time arrived at my ear, but like the sound of gunfire from far off. I immersed myself in a belief in the script under my pencil chiefly by pretending its theatrical production was not taking place.

The fact was, the show was improving. I reacted most to our difficulties, but through all the gunfire the work drove on, it was purposive, intelligent, tenacious, and done in conscience. No group of people could have worked harder; one of our stage managers said he had never seen a play rehearsed so mercilessly. What I thought of as being cooked in a pressure pot I saw was actually work in an experimental laboratory: every performance was under insatiable scrutiny, and Jessica's notes in the wink of her flashlight were devouring entire trees; Fred's and Arthur's critical findings on the script, the actors, the staging, the lights, the decor, the costumes, were routed back to this ear, that ear; scenes were rewritten and restaged, curtains and paintings and bedspreads vanished into limbo overnight and others fell in their place like manna, lights were rehung and their intensities altered, one wall of a set was abolished, another when built came on, and several hands were buying skirts for Annie; one task alone which took three weeks of crew rehearsal to complete, under Fred's bullwhip and Pete's soldierly execution, was the elimination of the curtain between scenes, so that the tide of activity I had witnessed from the bridge—swinging of sets, snatching and depositing of props, costume changes and scurrying of actors into position—could break and be gone in ten seconds of blackout instead of one minute under worklights. The premise which underlay all these labors for each of us was the winning of the audience. Every houseful was watched like a multiheaded behemoth; when spellbound it was soundless, when not it rustled its scaly fabrics and emitted little coughs, striking terror to our hearts; and those moments were without exception changed. I often wished it would cough itself to death, but by loving attention night after night we were learning to live with the behemoth in a state of blissful domestication. The question was, who was being tamed.

In its final phase I experienced the essential paradox of the production: the play grew more and more effective, and I felt less fulfilled as a writer.

14

I spent the remainder of the week like a monk in a cell, with my nose in the rewriting. Friends in town phoned me at the hotel, but with one exception I lacked the sense of leisure to dine out; Kevin invited me along on an afternoon tour of the art galleries, and I felt I could not afford it; Leah phoned from New York about another visit down to the show, but I said I would not have time even to talk to her. I myself saw no further performances until our last day in Washington.

I rewrote for the third time the ending of the first scene in the second act; I had gouged a lamentable hole in it when for reasons of romantic suspense I had rooted out the man's revelation of his love for his wife, no other matter was equal to fill it, but we kept trying. I had most of another scene on paper when Fred and Arthur came to say my arguments had persuaded them we should retain the original; I read them the new version, they were convulsed with laughter and deemed it brilliant, and we threw it in the wastebasket. I then reshaped the original, for the second time, to incorporate their points. We had another conference on the closing of the second act, in which we further clarified the issues at the curtain by reducing a complexity of motivations to one motive per character, and I rewrote it for the fourth time. Arthur then asked that it include a redeeming speech from the man enunciating his indebtedness to the girl; I rewrote it for the fifth time, and began a comparable—and I felt psychologically truer—speech about his marriage in the third act. Arthur returned the indebtedness speech the following day and said it was inadequate for what he intended, I invited him to try writing it, he declined, and I devoted twenty-four hours to truffling after truthful words in myself for material which was not mine but Arthur's; when I nosed out a usable source I wrote an aria of such length that a third of it had to be cut, but it brought tears to Arthur's eyes—he and Fred left a performance to hear it in my room—and he bore it back to the theater to show it to Hank, who then disliked what Arthur most liked in it. The sixth time around the scene went into the show and stayed, until the seventh time in Philadelphia. Fred and I had a separate session, in which I took notes on his survey of the rewriting chores remaining in the first and third acts. By the end of the week I was growing sick of the sight of these two alert, attractive, intelligent, articulate, tireless hounds of perfection, whose logic was irrefutable; I welcomed it much as a man with abdominal cramps welcomes an enema.

In the midst whereof, someone mailed me a morsel from a New York tabloid informing the public that because Annie was dominating the show we were doing "extensive revisions to beef up the Fonda part."

I had two conversations in my room that week which did not involve rewriting, but were aftermaths of my aborted move. One was with Arthur, on the comparative psychology of writers and directors, in which we arrived at a probable fallacy that writers had to be blabbermouths and directors had to be diplomats; Arthur said his one attempt to treat an actor with complete candor had been disastrous. The other conversation was with Fred, on whether we should accede to Hank's request that we import some top directors for a critical estimate of our condition. Hank had already intimated to me that a change in director might help, and I construed the imports as a step in that direction; I said to Fred that if Arthur okayed them for opinions only, I would too, but if it took us into the area of changing directors I would first see the show close. Fred said a change was not in question, and the topic and directors disappeared forever. We continued as we were, all dissatisfied, but walled in together by ten-foot-high contracts.

My one dinner out was with a free-lance writer on mental health, who conducted me to a press interview with a visiting psychologist from Warsaw. This took place over cocktails in the American Psychological Association headquarters, a building my wife had often set foot in, and bowing here to scholars in my identity as "Dr. Brenman's husband" I felt for the first time in weeks a breath of fresh air from some world outside of our show; the nation was still engaged in business other than manufacturing entertainment. I had new respect for my wife's profession since my anxiety attack, and the sight of her colleagues and their wives in a normal activity reminded me that I for one was no longer in my right mind, but in a hypnagogic trance induced by staring twenty-four hours a day at one glittering object, the show; it seemed to me that some such quasi-lunacy was inevitable in all show people on the road, sealed in one more spaceship in flight as their entire cosmos, unescapable from each other and without anchorage to anything else on earth, feeding on sleeping-pills and one another in an emotional cannibalism of violent antipathies and delusional love affairs, en route to the moon; but such speculation did not release me from the trance. The Warsaw psychologist journeyed back behind his iron curtain, and I journeyed back behind mine, to work upon the indebtedness aria.

Rumors of the show reached me in my cell. Arthur phoned to tell me Hank was commencing to play the profile I had asked for in the first act, as a "strange man" and a "sonofabitch"; Annie stopped in after a show to say Hank was "exciting," and giving her much more to react to; for two days running Fred reported Hank was "taking the stage," as evidenced in fewer laughs for the clown, and Arthur corroborated it, quoting Hank as saying on our penultimate day he thought "this was the right characterization"; one of the agents peripheral to the show visited it from New York and said, "What's everyone talking about, Hank takes stage!"

I was not unsuspicious of these reports, especially when on Saturday morning Arthur told me he had not slept all night as a result of an unhappy hour-and-a-half conversation with Hank over his midnight supper, so I went to inspect the last Washington matinee myself. My purpose was also to check on the ad libs Arthur and the actors had introduced in my absence, pending rewrites; the inanity of these so burned my ear I wanted to make a curtain speech listing them all for the audience, but I compromised by listing them for myself, to kill before our Philadelphia opening. Hank's matinee performance was improved, but not up to what I had been told, and I said so, whereupon Fred and Arthur—I think in apprehension of another paroxysm—invited me to stay in my room during the evening show, rewriting a first-act scene. I agreed.

But at the hotel I failed to reach by phone the friends I had been counter-inviting all week to meet me at our final performance; I stopped in on Arthur to announce I was obliged to go to the theater. I found him quite troubled: his wife and baby were now home from the hospital, inside that spaceship too of first motherhood, alone with the usual difficulties I was twice familiar with—his wife was giving the most gallant performance in our production—and Arthur was in an internal debate over which ship he should be in. I said it seemed obvious that a baby was more important than a show, and advised him to take off for an overnight visit. I left him inquiring by phone into train times, and I rode in a taxi back to the theater.

We had a large and responsive audience that night, and Hank played the opening act like a lion; it quelled the girl's comedy into proportion, and I could not refrain from running backstage in the intermission and up the stairs to his dressing-room, where half out of breath I told him I was seeing my man onstage for the first time and I hoped it felt good to him too. He said it did not, he could not see why the girl did not kick him out of her apartment, and wholly out of breath I went back to my friends. The show throughout was the best we had given. But one friend, who had seen the play prior to rewrites, touched off my own sense of our paradoxical improvement by observing not as a compliment that the audience was now "eating it up" and "what had I done to it"? I had no answer yet.

The minute the curtain came down the stagehands fell upon the set, tearing it to pieces under Pete's direction; the alley outside the theater was loaded like a wharf with crates waiting to be filled and shipped to Philadelphia. Our Washington adventure was done. Jessica, Annie, and I celebrated it by talking it over till four in the morning in Annie's room; in the familyless interior of this metallic missile I was sustaining myself on the blood of these girls, as they were on mine. We had lived in the nation's capital for three weeks, packed in on all sides by world-famous monuments and edificial wombs of current history, and seen the inside of nothing but our hotel rooms and the theater. And of ourselves. When Joey brought me my ticket I said it would be a very different train ride out of town from that coming in, we all knew each other much better now; Joey said impassively, "It was more pleasant the other way."

In this period we had whiplashed the show into a more appealing commodity, at a human and financial cost only half revealed in our statement of Washington operations; to economize on suspense and space, I include the comparable figures for our Philadelphia run as well:

	WASHINGTON	PHILADELPHIA
(*Performances*)	(20)	(21)
Box office receipts	$34,799.00	$72,020.75
Theater share	11,546.55	20,450.85
COMPANY SHARE	$23,252.45	$51,569.90

Expenses		
Salaries:		
Cast	$ 9,920.00	$13,753.96
Stage Managers	1,512.50	1,815.00
Company Manager	875.00	1,050.00
Press Agent	750.00	900.00
Production Secretary	425.00	510.00
Crew	5,872.50	6,930.00
Wardrobe and Dressers	614.63	737.55
Stagehands (taking in and out, and rehearsals)	5,597.34	5,594.31
Musicians (obligatory out of town)	1,009.41	1,127.68
Royalties:		
Author	—	4,054.50
Director	869.96	1,800.41
Publicity:		
Share of newspapers (exclusive of theater's share)	1,039.26	2,936.06
Photos and signs	219.48	766.91
Printing and promotion	74.26	541.35
Press expense	488.64	144.62
Subscription service, Theatre Guild	—	252.00
Departmental Expenses:		
Stage Manager	142.99	74.29
Electrical	1,276.42	687.06
Designer	227.23	—
Production Secretary	26.44	141.15
Property	—	170.77
Wardrobe	—	387.17
Carpenter	—	850.08

Rentals, electrical and sound equipment	2,765.00	2,184.00
Manager's expenses	50.00	50.00
Railroad	—	439.60
Box office	18.00	551.40
Transfer and cartage	—	3,357.90
Office expense	750.00	750.00
Out of town living expenses	1,740.00	1,710.00
Auditing	180.00	180.00
Payroll taxes	905.57	982.54
Insurance	968.82	968.82
Booking fees	212.50	225.00
Mercantile and General Business Tax	—	206.29
TOTAL EXPENSES	$38,530.95	$56,830.42
OPERATING PROFIT OR (LOSS)	$(15,278.50)	$(5,260.52)

The returns on the human cost were only half in.

In the morning I was seated in the lobby with my suitcase, when Edward G. Robinson and a stage actress walked into the hotel—arriving with another show—and Hank stepped out of the elevator. Robinson and he embraced each other, and the actress said, "How are you, Hank, are they fixing you up?" It was a glimpse of actors alone and in league, at the mercy of other talents, as all the talents were in this cogwork, like a model of human interdependence. When the rest of our company assembled we loaded ourselves and luggage into taxis, rode off to the depot, filed into another plush swivel-chaired car, and left Washington to its fate.

In my swivel chair I worked on first-act rewrites; we wanted them written, rehearsed, and in the show for our Philadelphia opening three days later. These concerned the man's offstage wife and Omaha background, which was not too intelligible, and the wife's absence from the action was a structural defect in the play. I was seeking a single incident to illuminate the marital past and have done with it, and by interrogating my companions in adjoining swivel chairs, found it: Fred contributed one element, Jessica another, and throwing in a third I wrote most of the passage between Washington and Philadelphia. My other accomplishment en route was to say at lunch, over a drop of egg on my sleeve, that I would lose my standing as one of the ten best-dressed men, which drenched the entire table in such a breaker of laughter that I have not ceased worrying about it since.

In the Philadelphia hotel—I loathed it on sight, a sumptuous ice palace of chrome and glass—I again stuck to my constitutional right to a double bed, an item which seemed to be disappearing out of American thought, or at least hostelry; my legs were long, and whatever spiritual agonies I suffered in this show, I intended to stretch them at night. The bellhop led me up and down and around to three rooms before we laid eyes on one, and I laid the rest of me on it to continue the rewrites. This room needed no protracted occupancy, it was hideous to begin with; fortunately, my eyeballs were now glazing over with prison purblindness. I rewrote all afternoon and through a room-service dinner—one steak, seven dollars, which I thought should have included a portion of the chrome and glass—and into the night, while outside in our theater somewhere the crew was once more laboring on sets and lights, and in some other den the cast was rehearsing with Arthur, now in from New York. Jessica reported from rehearsal to my room, to sit on phone books again and type multiple copies of what I had finished; meanwhile on the bed I thrust the falling bricks back in another scene, and rewrote the ad libs; and midnight found me ready to take the first-act material to Arthur and Fred. They relished it, luckily, since it was their appreciativeness and not inner compulsion which now was my source of work energy. With their acceptance of the rewrites, I at once phoned my wife from Arthur's room to say I would be driving to Massachusetts the following afternoon, for half a Christmas.

I had planned to attend the forenoon rehearsal of the new material, but I thought the hell with it, and by mid-morning I was in a rented car on the turnpike, racing north, with Philadelphia behind me. My one ambition, sprouting as of now, was to escape from show business forever—Fred said later he thought they would "never see me again"—and live at home as uneventfully as a carrot in the ground; it would be another three weeks, but as we neared New York my heart was breaking into a run for Stockbridge like a horse that smells the stable; my mind was not on success or failure, but on how many months were in the next twenty days. (Hank was asking for another two weeks on the road: I told Fred I thought it a splendid idea, and I would be in Stockbridge.) Yet my entire anatomy was possessed solely by the materials of the show. I was driving because I was good for nothing else, not even reading; a glassed-in day of train rides with my eyes unseeing on a book had seemed like a sentence to torture; I needed some sense of rudimentary action and control, if only of a steering wheel. I drove for five hours with the window open to the winter air, the sunlight, the plaidwork of farmlands, the pine and white birch and hemlock mountainsides piling up toward home, it was all like mother's milk. I walked into the house three hours early, and my family climbed me like a soldier home from the wars.

I was not inside twenty minutes when Hollywood called: the studio that had fired me wanted to hire me. I was at this time uncertain of what I would earn, if anything, out of *Two for the Seesaw*. But an old concept re-emerging in me from the buried years I had spent as a poet was that of the "serious" man, an inappropriate term by which I did not mean gifted, intelligent, responsible, indefatigable, or any of the other attributes possessed in a high degree by the executive talents I had now watched work and admired in a fair sampling of theatrical media, movies, television, stage; I meant something much more moral, I meant what Lucifer said, "I will not serve." I meant by serious a touch of madness, the inward eye, in scientist, artist, saint, men who exemplified a New Englander's saying, "The things for which we visit a man were done alone in the dark and the cold." The men I had met in show business, unlike the nincompoops I met in fictional accounts of it, were extraordinary by any standards: but all their work was done collaboratively in the behemoth's mouth. It seemed to me this was not a habitat in which to find serious men as so defined (I remembered the great Viennese actor who was asked to play Prospero, and after pondering it for days said no, because "to play Prospero one must be not only a great actor but a great man: and whether a great man would *become* an actor. . . .") and I was revising my idea of myself downwards from the heroic level I dwelt on in fantasy. Fifteen years earlier, when my work consisted of unpublished poems and a magazine asked me to change a word in one, I would not change the word; the poem went unpublished; it was a far cry to the present spate of rewriting to please, and I wondered what had become of that young Lucifer. I felt this of all of us, that in outgrowing his guardian angelship and becoming reasonable citizens we had all lost some religious component in ourselves, and this component was the difference between art and entertainment. These were ponderous considerations, especially at long-distance rates, and there seemed to be some confusion in them of divine purpose and personal obstinacy, but on a level below any need to justify it I knew that to work further with accomplices in the behemoth's mouth meant a diminishment of myself; I was not hireable now by any wing of the entertainment industry for a million dollars, and tactfully conveyed as much to the studio executive. I decided I would send my wife back to work instead.

For a day and a half I visited as an alien in our house. My

wife had been valiantly shouldering weeks of winter illnesses in our boys without my aid or knowledge, the daily domestic routines I had hungered to return to were unenterable, and the people I loved most in the world seemed furthest from mind; my head was addled, I could not bear to be away from the collaborators I could not bear to be with. We celebrated a spurious Christmas for the boys on the twenty-fourth, with an outlay of gifts for them I had not helped buy, under a young pine out of our woods I had not cut or helped decorate. Our one-year-old had adopted his grandpa as a father, and our four-year-old was in a weeks-long mourning of wretched destructiveness; I endeavored to explain my coming absence to that small head as the last of my business trips to make money on which we would live for a long time without separations. Money or not, I knew this had to be true: the life of show business I was inflicting on all of us was subhuman. The company meanwhile had scattered to their own homes for Christmas Eve; I phoned Arthur and Annie to offer greetings, heard reports of more eruptions, and among our yuletide cards found one from an ex-producer consoling us on my being in "a murderers' business." On Christmas Day I left my wife in bed racked with a bronchial illness, and drove back to Philadelphia.

I found my way to our theater there, another cavernous barn, to witness the tail end of an afternoon run-through with Annie whispering her part; her throat had been troubling her for several days. With her audibility in question, we gathered three hours later in the populous lobby for our opening. Arthur and Fred were nerved up and on the prowl among our incoming audience, which included the customary sprinkling of our agents, theater folk, and other advance spies from New York, but my mood was oddly calm; since my assignment a week ago to the role solely of writer, I felt much less responsibility for what occurred onstage. I sat through the show in a protective boredom. The performance was lusterless—with Annie audible but weak, and Hank playing on a level midway between his opening and closing work in Washington—but the script as reshaped with Fred and Arthur more expertly held the audience, and the curtain calls were encouraging.

Afterwards our entire company adjourned to a restaurant across the alley, for midnight drinks and steaks, while we awaited the reviews which would corroborate or subvert our sense of what we had accomplished in Washington. The first reaction came in over the radio, and the roomful of clatter, ice-cubes, voices, silverware, suddenly stilled: in silence we listened to an impromptu chat by a commentator who in comparing the two roles said, "I don't mean Fonda's part is inferior," and Hank from the back of the room called across me to the radio, "You just mean it's inferior," but the commentary was enthusiastic. The first newspaper review was taken by Fred over the phone, and relayed piecemeal by him to the room; it was also favorable.

By noon the next day I had bought the three local newspapers and clipped the reviews, and a day or two later mailed them to my wife.

15

HENRY T. MURDOCK's review in the *Philadelphia Inquirer*—as phoned to us it had concluded with a paragraph commendatory of Arthur's work, omitted in print presumably for lack of space—was headed "Fonda Star in Off-Beat Love Story":

> *The two-character play is a rarity in the theatre and an even greater rarity is one which can be carried off without undue recourse to "gimmicks" and stunts, mainly revolving around Alexander Graham Bell's invention.*
>
> *Making his debut as playwright (although he has some screenwriting credits), William Gibson carries off his self-*

induced problem with great wit and ability in "Two for the Seesaw" which opened last night at the Forrest.

To be sure, the telephone is a busy "prop," but in this case Gibson has used it mainly as an extension of the dialogue between his two characters, a continuance of their approach to an off-beat love story and therefore a valid device.

One gets the impression that Gibson wrote a two-character play not just as a display of virtuosity but because, given his plot, and given a pair of players of such force and resource as Henry Fonda and Anne Bancroft, two characters were all that were needed.

And since we are dealing in pairs tonight, two impressive debuts are registered in the play. In addition to Gibson's contribution, which is a skillful excursion in a paradoxical display of hard-boiled tenderness, Miss Bancroft, heading for Broadway for the first time, lights up the stage with her funny, explosive, warm-hearted gamine heroine.

In no way is this intended to suggest that she "steals the show" from Fonda. No one can take such liberties with that lean and sometimes saturnine master of underplaying. In many ways Fonda has the less sympathetic role and one might question the playwright's conclusion that his invasion of the life of an open-hearted, generous, down-to-earth Bronx girl has left her any less mixed-up than she was before.

Nevertheless, Fonda makes his points with skill and maintains his full share in the duet delivered by the ill-matched lovers.

Miss Bancroft's role and performance can best be described through a bit of plot recital. Fonda plays an Omaha lawyer who flees from his wife of 10 years because of her possessiveness and the indulgence of a wealthy woman who can buy a career for her mate. He has become tired of eternal acceptance; dubious of his own merits.

In New York the first person he talks to in a month is Gittel, a frustrated ballet dancer who doesn't know she is frustrated, who is just as indulgent though probably less possessive than his wife.

For 29 years she has lived a knock-about life, collected a serious ulcer, a parade of "affairs" and a vocabulary that makes one's hair stand straight up on end. At the same time she has maintained a sort of innocence and loveability, both of which, plus the ulcer, the affairs and the vocabulary are beautifully emphasized in Miss Bancroft's performance.

So these two souls, so dependent in the face of their asserted independence and unwillingness to accept favors, battle their way to the theory that, when there is a call to obligations, the verb "to help" is right after the verb "to love."

Jerry Gaghan's review in the *Philadelphia Daily News* was headed " 'Two for the Seesaw' at Forrest":

The customary pitfalls of the two-character play are skillfully eluded in "Two for the Seesaw," which opened last evening at the Forrest.

Author William Gibson shrewdly keeps his two protagonists in view nearly all of the time, which avoids those dread moments of waiting for you know who can come on.

There is also wide enough difference in his two types to make their amatory play and conflict crackle all evening until it sputters out at the finish. And seldom has that fearsome instrument of theatrical exposition—the telephone—been put to happier use.

The players—Henry Fonda and Anne Bancroft—spend a good part of the running time with Mr. Bell's handy gadget, but all to sound purpose and to expedite rather than clutter the stage doings.

Briefly, "Two for the Seesaw" is the story of a pair of lonely, mixed-up people in New York. They meet and have a fleeting fling at what passes for love, which the playwright would have us believe, results in a better understanding of themselves.

There are moments of rollicking interchange and perceptive passages. But there are also lagging, padded stretches and some bits of stupid bed-pan humor.

Fonda's intelligent grasp of a role makes credible the self-tormented attorney from Omaha. The playwright hasn't too clearly defined the reason for this gentleman's flight from wifely and in-law domination to lose himself in the metropolis.

Fonda even makes you bridge the basic gap—that an attorney of Brooks Bros. convictions could have ever gotten involved with the Bohemian babe from the Bronx in the first place.

Miss Bancroft's profane, broken-down ballerina with the heart of gold is not only a different level socially, but histrionically.

In contrast to Fonda's repressed style, she mugs unashamedly and ranks as one of the year's busiest performers.

Max de Schauensee's review in the *Evening Bulletin* was headed "Henry Fonda and Anne Bancroft Star in 'Two for the Seesaw' ":

Nothing terribly important happens in William Gibson's two-character play, "Two for the Seesaw," which opened at the Forrest last night. Nevertheless, Mr. Gibson has written an often searching and taut "slice of life."

After a first act that seemed juvenile while establishing the two characters—a lawyer who hails from the West and is wandering about New York and a Jewish seamstress from the Bronx—the play suddenly becomes adult in the second act, as intense emotion and completely believable revelations of character hold the stage.

The first stage, as the actors scatter profanities like toy pistol shots, hurl objects across the room and blithely call each other on the telephone at 5 in the morning, gave no indication of the emotional marrow that forms much of the play's later serious moments.

Fortunately, it is the big scenes of "Two for the Seesaw" that find Gibson working at his best and writing pages that have a sense of unusual reality and even superb urgency. The climax he reaches during the second act is one of considerable impact.

Like all two-character plays, "Two for the Seesaw" depends enormously on the brilliance and credibility of the performances. Gibson has been fortunate, for Anne Bancroft as the tough, almost illiterate, but big-hearted girl from the Bronx, and Fonda as the confused lawyer, teetering on the edge of divorce and looking for some meaning to his life, come through with remarkable fine performances.

It is a question, however, whether the neurotic, well-educated Jerry Ryan would have been attracted and allowed himself to become deeply involved with a girl whose surface was so vulgarly crude as that of Gittel Mosca.

It is a triumph on Miss Bancroft's part that she is able to enlist the gradual warmth and even nobility. Nothing that Miss Bancroft has shown in her numerous movie roles gave any indication of the talent she displays here.

The telephone is unusually prominent; with only two characters, it has to be. Thus, a third character (Fonda's estranged wife) is practically brought to life and given dimension through telephonic and actual conversations.

It is Fonda's indecision and shilly-shallying between Miss Bancroft and the woman he has loved that forms the theme of Gibson's little saga.

The dialogue often contains the ring of truth, but the

author (probably to obtain contrast) also indulges in a lusty realism of expression that borders on the unattractive. The frequent profanity also proved that laughter can be easily obtained from an audience.

It is nice to report that Gibson's play ends in the only way it possibly could from a realistic standpoint, for Cinderella and Prince Charming rarely make out successfully in everyday life, where the cards are stacked against them.

Like its title, Gibson's piece seesaws up and down from brilliance to mediocrity. Fortunately, the "ups" are what you are likely to remember as you walk up Chestnut St. from the Forrest Theatre.

Arthur Penn's direction, if not always unmindful of the audience, is, on the whole, excellent. George Jenkins' two-room set with his skyline background, proves effective for this tale of emotional confusion, generosity and relinquishment.

16

My experience of external events in what remained of our Philadelphia sojourn I could distill almost in a sentence: I lived on my chenille bedspread, was ill, then lived under it, and in both locations rewrote, after which we opened in New York. It was internal events I was really noting. The fact was unblinkable, after such reviews, that the hammering my script and head had undergone at the hands of Arthur, Fred, and Hank had issued in a much better play, and certainly one more to the behemoth's taste. That it was not more to mine was interpretable, even by me, solely in terms of my sulking vanity; but I believed a deeper meaning for me also lay in this paradox. Henceforth I was to give much less thought to the show as show, and much more to its place in the layout of my life.

One evening when I stood with Fred watching the audience roar with laughter he asked me what it felt like hearing my lines accomplish that, and I answered truthfully it felt like nothing. It had not been so with our first audiences. An alienation from my own work was setting in, and with it a benumbment. Arthur threw in more business and I threw in more lines, like fish to seals, but I took no pleasure in the bark of new laughs now, it was an easy game of which I rather disapproved. I was not yet so numb as to be insensible to pain, and a dozen trivial changes made in rehearsal for reasons I could guess at—rearrangements of lines to sharpen laughs, synonymic substitutions for immediate clarity, dilutions of the girl's promiscuity and displeasing profanities—stuck in my ear at each performance like pins; but I was growing too demoralized, and too sick in my bones of our incessant conversations, to argue every minuscule item. I saw my own needs as unreasonable, they called for nothing less than the bismarckian control of every square inch I enjoyed in writing a poem, and the hope of attaining this by working through the temperaments of others was lunacy. My task was to dissemble my lunacy until I escaped from my keepers on January 16.

I made a final pass at the staging after our second performance in Philadelphia, which was so soporific it undid my boredom. The next morning I ate breakfast alone in the ornate reaches of the hotel dining-room, waited for Fred and Arthur to awaken, and ate a second breakfast with them, over which I recapitulated my list of acting and directing problems. I went backstage before curtain that evening to solicit pace of Hank and Annie individually. The show picked up, for whatever reason, but I scrutinized this performance from the third row instead of our usual roost at the back of the house: the reviewer's charge that Annie mugged was just, while at close quarters Hank was most real and moving. Our destination was one of the smallest theaters in New York, and I was concerned that in these out-of-town circus-tents our need for a big show was still exacting from Annie an excessive performance which might mar the Broadway debut of what we all now knew was a remarkable talent. I spoke to her of the mugging, her reaction as usual was blankly to have no idea what I meant, and I promised her two dozen notes in detail to be made from the third row the following night; I talked it over also with Arthur, who had a dinner conference with her beforehand; Annie then let me sit through the show with pad and pencil in hand, and not one instance of mugging to note. I made instead a half-dozen small notes for Hank—it was our best show to date—and took them to him in his dressing-room, my last formal act of opinion on the production.

Despite the improved reviews, our anxieties were on the rise. The two days following our opening I spent in good part listening to Arthur and Fred on streamlining the text in the third act, after which I took pencil to its first scene. I finished it again—but not for the last time—on Saturday morning, and moved into the penultimate scene; I bogged down on this in the afternoon, walked to the theater for a critical look at it late in the matinee, and went back to the pages in my room; I conferred again that night with Arthur and Fred until two-thirty. It was a more sour conversation, at least in my mouth. I was growing balky about suggestions for content which, increasingly alien to my body of experience, felt like merely logical and slippery notions for theatrical moments; they were no doubt valuable as such, and even called for to reconcile the contradictions between the man as written and as acted, but I had my own slickness to be afraid of, I had let my head forfeit too much of my original intent, and my bowels were coming belatedly to the rescue by finding our confederate logic more and more indigestible. Sunday morning I continued the rewriting on my bed, where I took two phone calls, from Annie and Fred inside the hotel; each came up for a talk prior to leaving for rehearsal. Annie was in trouble with an unfillable hole in a scene where we had removed a huge brick, and I said

I would write more fill, though it would do no good. Fred had two points: he was on edge that the rewrites were not coming out of me fast enough, and he thought Arthur was depressed because I no longer seemed to "stand behind" the show. I said I was rewriting as fast as I could dig up words I was not ashamed of, and denied feeling I had "sold the play out to the philistines." But I spent too many hours that afternoon mulling over his second point to deliver much on his first. I worked on with what little focus I could call back, and when the hotel air waxed too groggy I phoned home, talked a bit with my wife and my older boy, and took up the rewriting with a new burst of lack of enthusiasm. Jessica then phoned from rehearsal—we had planned to see a movie that night with Annie, my first in months—to say Arthur's orders were for me to stay in my room and work; I hit the ceiling, and told her to inform Arthur I did not take such orders. Fred then phoned from inside the hotel and asked how I felt, and I said furious, I would go to movies whenever I saw fit, and moreover I thought his morning visit ill-timed, however it may have discharged his tension it had kept me from working half the day; Fred said he was sorry if it was an error, he had just come from a comparable run-in with Arthur in rehearsal, and he was sure there was a misunderstanding about the movie; I said I thought this brain trust had to be very careful lest our anxieties grow reciprocally destructive. Jessica then phoned from rehearsal to say that she had misquoted Arthur while grinding an axe of her own, it was Annie who "shouldn't" go to the movie because of her throat; I said I liked that better, and Annie could make her own decision. The three of us went to the movie and no harm was done, except by the men who had made the movie, but the whole day seemed skinless with exposed nerves.

I awoke on Monday morning with my wife's bronchitis in my windpipe. My head felt as brainless as a rock; I was already worried over my inability to pry any interest out of it for the rewriting at hand. For both reasons, I canceled a breakfast date with John Houseman. (Houseman was in town with a Shakespeare play, and we had been endeavoring for days to find an hour of leisure in common; three years earlier in Hollywood when I was impatient with scene revisions he had said, "Wait until you get into a Philadelphia hotel with one of your plays"; here I was, hungering to swap theater nightmares with him, but I settled for a few phone scraps in which he told me that with a seeming success we were "having it easy.") Phoning Jessica, I asked her to shop for and bring me a couple of quarts of fruit juice, to cure my symptoms, and a fifth of rye, to dull them. I kept to my room all day and into the night, working on the penultimate scene; my only distractions were an afternoon meal alone in the grill, and an evening exhibit of the love act in a window opposite by an ill-matched couple whom I judged to be a speedboat manufacturer and a call girl; after their performance and ours, Arthur, Fred, and I met to confer further on the scene I thought I had finished finishing two days before. I now made an attempt to swallow our most indigestible piece of collective logic. It was a call for a half-dozen explicit touches of "team spirit"—the man urging the bed-ridden girl to "join the team" by arising—throughout the scene; quite apart from the fact that I was in no mood to write paeans to the team spirit, the notion did violence to my palate, but two days later I delivered the lines as requested. They came out so involuntarily rancid that Arthur never gave them to the actors, and Fred said teasingly I wasn't a "team man," I was a "loner."

On the closing night of the year I finished rewriting the penultimate scene; it had been a racking effort against my illness, and I was finding the material increasingly dead as a mutton to feel my way into. Fred and Arthur came from the theater to hear it, and thought it one of the best things in the play. (Two days later we put it into the show; four days later we threw it out again, it was not the answer to our streamlining needs.) Fred had planned a New Year's Eve party for our company at the Variety Club, another after-hours refuge for theater folk, but with me confined to the hotel corridors he rerouted the party into his room. It was a gesture I much appreciated; I phoned my wife at midnight, and sat drinking and talking with the others in Fred's room for three hours into the new year.

I spent the first day of 1958 in bed, my cawing throat, drippy nose, and chest rumble worsening; Arthur came in before the matinee to make third-act cuts with me, and I rewrote some second-act passages through another room-service dinner and the evening. I was no better the next day, but I wrapped up my head and took a taxi to the theater to watch the new penultimate scene rehearsed. It was performed that night, but I did not see it: I ate in the dining-room with Jessica—I felt if I died in the hotel, as seemed likely, she was the only person who would take time to bury my body—and retired to my bed to finish one of the second-act scenes for the fourth time, or expire in the attempt, before my wife's arrival in the morning. So ended our sixtieth day.

My wife knocked at my door at six a.m., and my flesh and spirit went gratefully into her hands. We rode together to the theater that day to catch a rehearsal, and walked in on Fred pacing the lobby in a white quiver: we said it seemed early in the day to be pacing, and learned he had just come from a difference of opinion with Hank onstage in which everyone thought everyone intended to hit everyone. In the subsequent course of work Annie became nauseated; she was dismissed to her dressing-room, rehearsal suspended, and a doctor summoned. This interruption, like my mucus, was construed by her colleagues as temperament, but either way the human toll was real and mounting, for all of us. Hank now saw his acceptance of the play as a by-product only of having "fallen in love with Gittel"; I had watched men more harrowed by daily misery, but not outside of walls and responsibly functioning;

I thought the price his soul was paying for this piece of entertainment was exorbitant for anything short of paradise, and his stamina in continuing was laudable. Annie's soul was made of leather, but her body was not: the day after our Philadelphia opening a boil in her throat had been lanced, and the next afternoon a doctor at rehearsal had ordered her back to the hotel in a state of exhaustion; cross-legged postures in the play had also extruded a hernia in one of her knee-pits, and she now rehearsed and acted with it encased in an elastic bandage. When at dinner I suggested a rehearsal policy of sparing Annie's throat by having someone read her lines, Arthur said frostily such an arrangement would "not be at all helpful"; the toll on Arthur I felt as bleakness, he was our only male without even the intermittent presence of a wife to grace his solitude, he was barren of his baby, and I sensed in him a recession of body warmth from everyone, as though bled of all bestowals except sheer intelligence. Fred like a good producer usually kept his fox in his entrails, but his exterior calm was becoming paler by the week, and through the infrequent cracks in it I glimpsed the chewing; apart from his own career, he was responsible for $80,000 of other people's money. Our stage managers were drawn taut as rubber bands, working through flu, bursitis, and what not, and even Jessica—whose fate in no way was in the scales, her job ended on opening night no matter what—was hanging on only by her teeth. As for me, Arthur said months later I seemed to him "ravaged," compulsively lashing out, and less and less effective in conferences; I knew and said I was having the most odious experience of my life, and every corpuscle of me was in recoil.

I studied the text of our evening show with my own eye: I had not seen it for a week, time was running out, and I was determined to rewrite now to satisfy the remnant shreds of my personal judgment alone. With Annie ill the performance was not up to our best, though my wife thought it much improved over Washington—the playwright who had written me there so generously said the betterment of the script since was "fantastic"—and we went back to the dressing-rooms for her to compliment the actors. My wife asked Hank whether it now felt more comfortable, Hank said not one moment onstage felt comfortable, she asked what made it worthwhile then, was it money, and Hank said no amount of money could make it worthwhile, he had not worked with such unactable writing since so-and-so, "another novelist"; and I escaped upstairs to the rest of the cast. Still another playwright was in attendance that night, and Fred asked me to join Arthur and him in picking his brains in the hotel grill. I was so brimful of the team spirit I could not swallow another drop, however precious: at each glimpse of Fred and Arthur bent on a conference I went into semi-shock, my eyes crossed, I saw them distorted into ominous spooks, and I never heard them knock on my door without wanting to hide under the bed; I had not dreaded such ogres since I was Jack on the beanstalk. So I pleaded my illness and did hide in bed, and they conferred with the other playwright, who was in better shape, until four in the morning.

I was on my deathbed the next noon when Arthur and Fred came to bring me their pickings; with my wife present to protect me, I told them before they were quite seated that I would listen to anything, but I knew exactly what and how I wanted to rewrite for myself and I intended to proceed to it regardless. This somewhat dampened the sparks of communication. I did listen, though I surmised they departed with half their suggestions tactfully unspoken, and I was incurious. My wife absented herself from the room that afternoon shopping, and that evening at the theater, while I stayed in bed rewriting a scene in the second act for the fifth time and one in the third act for the fourth time. Afterwards my wife told me of a disagreement she and Fred had at the theater: he regretted my obstinacy, I was too unwilling to experiment with material this way and that, and some shows had been on the road for as much as a year, being experimented with constantly. I was now convinced I was in the hands of creatures from outer space.

My skull had been in a bind of low fever all week, and when on Sunday morning it approached a hundred and one my wife thought it time to call in a doctor; he diagnosed my complaint as bronchitis without pneumonic complications, and put me on a diet of aureomycin. I continued working in bed throughout the day and evening, on the new penultimate scene to replace the new penultimate scene, with time off only for a visit Annie and Jessica paid us after rehearsal. Monday morning saw me through the thick of it, and at three o'clock in the afternoon Jessica hurried the new pages over to rehearsal, for inclusion in performance that evening. I caught a nap, got out of bed and dressed, downed a malted for dinner, and went with my wife to the theater.

The moment the taxi neared it I was singed by a fit of anxiety; we entered backstage to wish the actors luck, and Annie confessed anxiety; we proceeded out to the audience, and met Fred haunting the rear aisle in anxiety. Our jitters seemed to be self-fueled now, no longer prompted by realities: the show was looking better, the box office was thriving on word of mouth, and though in this performance the newly learned dialogue was scrambled, the line of the third act at last had the unimpeded drive we were after. Our audience included the producer and cast of another show in town, and my nerves soaked in their enthusiasm backstage after the curtain. (It must have cost them something: their own production was in trouble, they were in the act of swapping directors in mid-struggle, in our hotel I saw the authors—two of the best comedy writers in television—riding the elevator together mute as sleepwalkers, and having suffered all we suffered and worse, they closed in New York after four performances.) That night for the first time I glimpsed a crack of daybreak beyond our spotlights.

I was more on my feet the next morning and my wife, having overstayed by two days her scheduled return to our boys, took a morning train home. I had now rewritten what I myself needed, and I turned to a dozen scraps of dialogue Fred had requested for further explicitness; each of these straws felt like lifting a butt log. In the afternoon I went to rehearsal, where I listened to Annie in a deadlock with Arthur over some matter I neither could nor cared to follow, until Arthur called me onstage to insert a "more explicit" line, this straw being the last: in my esthetic, explicitness was death: and the words welled out of me in a stammer of asperity, I said the point was explained three lines later, we could keep the damned audience waiting for three lines, and the practice of rendering what I wrote "untrue" for the sake of a facile clarity was a "deep grievance" I had with the production throughout. Arthur said in a low voice the line was not important and walked back to the actors, and Fred sat to reason with me, saying the passage as it stood not only kept the audience waiting but misled it meanwhile, and I said very well, they could put in their seven words, which they did, while I left the stage whose creative fires seemed only to bring my lunacy to a boil. I apologized to Arthur a half-hour later for having said a "hurtful" thing, adding it had much more to do with me than with him. I made a request of my own to Pete and Fred late that afternoon: I had written the final scene of the play against the man's room stripped of everything except his typewriter and suitcase; to speed up the set change we had been letting more and more furniture stand in it, which destroyed the bleak mood I wanted, and I said the stripping was more essential than the speed-up. Pete said he would work out an attack of stagehands to deliver both. I was taken aback with pleasure to see it happen a few hours later in performance; the crew stripped the man's room so enthusiastically they even made off with his suitcase, and that night my character went back to Nebraska without his clothes, but the bleakness and something in me were restored.

On Wednesday afternoon I completed the last of Fred's requested lines, and locked up the typewriter like a rattlesnake. I sat looking at it with a dead eye: I was done, I could not believe it (and it turned out not to be true). I had never before been so exacerbated and drained by a stretch of writing, and for a comprehensible reason, it was not what I called my "own" work: in my own work, poem, novel, play, I began with an internal dilemma and unlocked it in the dreaming and wording, an act which liberated my energies, and thus day after day replenished and refreshed me; but this brand of rewriting was external, at best unrelated to and at worst a diminution of the conceptual origins of the play, and though done to solve undeniable problems, had sucked my bones dry. I celebrated the drouth by skipping the matinee. Watching that evening's performance it dawned on me that I could flee Philadelphia earlier than Saturday midnight; after the show, at the Variety Club with the Coes, Arthur, and Annie, I told Fred that if he had no objections I would leave Friday. Fred bowed his head in a kind of assent. I was by now in such a state of noxious indigestion that everything my eye took in at this theater hangout grated in my gizzard: in my years as a beer-joint pianist I had lost my minimal tolerance for night haunts, and seeing now the wanderings in and out of personnel from other shows in town—aging romantic leads, and peroxide blondes in blue-jeans with bearded lads in bear-like sweaters, and lostlings of neither sex, blessed faces and bodies living hard and losing their looks, all burning with some inner torch of narcissistic talent not three in a thousand would be unbetrayed by, and in the name of which they let go the daily bread of commonplace life to starve like exotic birds of passage in a wasteland of hotels, dingy make-up rooms, and night air—I felt I was in the presence of a cultural tragedy, like the dust-bowl migrations. Oddly, I was the only one in the room dying of maladjustment. In answering a question of Annie's about the new lines, I said brightly I had written them "just to keep the producer happy"; Fred gazed at me for a minute and then cuttingly told me off, saying he didn't like my manner, his requests for lines were made to protect my script, and I should not be contemptuous of my audience, they were smarter than I thought. I agreed with him, I felt I was getting difficult to take. I went to bed that night and lay awake for hours, anxiously phosphorescent, until I put on the lamp to study a kitchen snapshot of my boys' faces for half an hour, and sustained by those two muffins at length slept.

In the morning Arthur phoned me with a tidbit—*The Miracle Worker* had won an award for the best television play of the year—and Fred paid me a visit to chat, in the course of which we agreed we would come into New York to mixed reviews, as a modest success. I was still in a paradoxical knot over how the show could feel better when I felt worse, and I took the occasion to tell Fred that no matter how I kicked against it I was perversely grateful for his keeping at me, on the other hand my obstinacy was how I had safeguarded my talent for twenty-five years; Fred said I must realize he was responsible to many people for delivering a show, and he thought we had nevertheless not lost hold of the script; I concurred. It was something of a miracle that in our plunge through star-crossed space we had kept our bearings at all, and in some dim backroom of my mind I knew I was deeply indebted for it to two remarkable ogres. I spent the day unwinding, and making farewell addresses. I had lunch with Annie having breakfast, and enjoyed the luxury of companionless attendance at a matinee of another play, though I watched it with a glass eye, and ate a valedictory dinner with Arthur, and watched our evening performance with two glass eyes, and told Hank in his dressing-room I would see him next in New York—he said briefly, "I'll be there"—and rode back to the hotel with Annie, and left a so-long note in Jessica's silent door, and hiding from a midnight repast with Fred's lawyer and agent, packed my bags for the morning. I slept that night as untroubledly as a crocodile.

I was out of the hotel Friday by eight-thirty, and on the train by nine. I sat once more in a swivel chair, but this time solitary, and disguised behind a fresh copy of the New York *Herald Tribune* as a contented businessman; my sensations were those of a released convict, determined henceforth to go straight. In New York I made a beeline by taxi out of Penn Station, and then impatiently hung around Grand Central for an hour until it was time to board a train for the town of Hudson. I was to be picked up there by car, an involved arrangement made to get me home seven hours earlier than the Stockbridge train; it was our sixty-eighth day, and I would have sold a finger for every hour. I devoted some mulling on this trip to the riddle of my paradox, but it was to take me many weeks, and the writing of a cathartic log, to come to terms with it. The facts however were now all in, and the experience was essentially behind me; win, lose, or draw, our Broadway reception was for me no longer a goal, but an irrelevance.

I did not enjoy myself cast as the playwright uttering his traditional outcry, that it was "not my play" on the stage; I felt as though this line too had been written by someone else. It was not my play, and it was. The writer is a primary artist: where nothing was, he ordains a world. If he creates it in literary form his work is then done, he need only find a way into print. If however he has committed the indiscretion of creating it in dramatic form he must find a way onto a stage, and it is at this point that his work acquires three species of co-workers. The first is in the realm of economics. The producer, like the publisher, must be persuaded that accepting the work will not be sheerly an eleemosynary act: but a book can be manufactured for a few thousand dollars, and the risk is minimized by fifty others in the course of a publisher's year; a play cannot be mounted for less than a fortune, which is subscribed by a host of partners to whom the producer is answerable, and it is gambled on a single throw of the dice. The writer here becomes part and parcel of a complex business organization formed to manufacture and sell one article of merchandise; and any producer who viewed his function as merely to be the playwright's coachman would deposit everyone in the ditch. When a producer buys a play it is thus spoken of as "his" play, and not improperly. The second species is in the sphere of the secondary arts. The playwright must have interpretive talents; they are secondary because their concerted work is made possible only by his solitary work beforehand. But the art of the theater is not one of reciting his words, and although in theory the talents who undertake to recreate his world onstage by other means, flesh, movement, color, are embodiers and deliverers of his vision, they all in fact deliver two substitutes: their vision of his vision, and the totality of themselves. These substitutes are to his interpreters what the writer's experience was initially to him, the raw material and fount, out of which and only which their work if honest can spring; the director cannot stage a play or aspects of it, the actor cannot characterize a role or aspects of it, that he has not made his own. When a director or star agrees to do a play it is also spoken of as "his" play, and not improperly. It is not excessive to say that each of their plays and the writer's play often have much in common. But they differ in subterranean ways by the lifetime of private experience, temperament, values, and hopes each collaborator brings with him onto the stage; what is rehearsed is thus several plays, no participant enjoys the freedom to create his own play uninterfered with, and the tug-of-war which ensues is an attempt by each to pull the others into his; it is in effect a class struggle to see who will own the means of esthetic production. This struggle of esthetes takes place in the economic ring of the producer's play. In practice, identities overlap like multi-colored paint: the producer functions as quasi-artist and esthetic critic, and the artists all criticize the producer's business sense; everyone wants to make art, and everyone wants to make money, and each goal is confounded with the other. The third species of co-workers is encountered thus in the shape of the behemoth-bank which contains the money, and the art becomes that of shaking it out. When a spectator sits to watch a play it is never spoken of as "his" play, but it properly should be: none of the active hands so tyrannically molds the materials as does the behemoth's passive posterior, which has haunted the work from its inception, and in no other art or business is it couchant in the center of the workshop. The manufacturer who undertakes washing-machines and sees eyecups come off his conveyor belt is seldom successful; anyone in the theater can name plays which began as solemn drama and ended profitably—and conceivably better—as rowdy comedies, in collaboration with the genius of the audience. The co-workers being thus assembled, the medium is complete. The several plays already in work now struggle for survival in the behemoth's mouth. What it coughs at, however precious to its creators, disappears from the stage; and the collective labor is given over to marrying as much of the art to as much of the money as talent and time and talk can effect. Talk is the one bridge that connects the several plays, the talk is ceaseless, and the material under scrutiny begins its shrinkage to the dimensions of what is verbalizable. In this shrinkage the writer's play undergoes a special gain, for which he loves his helpers, and a special loss, for which he hates them. It is the one play of the lot wrested in the dark and the cold out of the nothingness antecedent to language, and its source and first preconscious shape lie in inarticulate depths, as profound as its author is gifted. The words in which he clothes it for public appearance are a kind of skin, the nervework of which ramifies deep in an unseen body; this body is the secret torso of his experience as a man, conscious and unconscious, idiosyncratic and typical; the writing is mottled with the blindness and the insights of a lifetime. In one word, the play is, in the image of its maker, imperfect. In literary forms the author is entitled to his characteristic imperfections, including the right occasionally to bore his reader with a mammoth paragraph, but in the theater boredom is the one disease fatal to the behemoth, without whose viability there is no play; the collective logic to which the writer's play is subjected aims therefore at ruthlessly perfecting it. In palpable measure, given responsible colleagues and a flair in the author for rewriting under pressure, this is attained. What his play gains is clarity, appeal, celerity, impact, and other virtues arrivable at in open intelligent discussion. The crooked tree is planed straight; what it loses are individualistic imperfections often organic to its total character and connected by underground roots to buried treasure, a multiplicity of non-verbalizable meanings in both the playwright and the audience. What the audience never knows cannot hurt it, but the playwright suffers the paradoxical experience of seeing his work improve by becoming poorer, and amid the congratulations of all, deduces he is losing his mind. That the collective perfecting of the script lifts it progressively nearer to a surface of commercial gloss need be willed by none of the participants; the surface wills them. At another remove, this is true even in the amateur theater, but the professional enterprise is a—let us say—$80,000 roller-coaster ride on a track that leads in one direction; time is brief, at no point can the group call a halt to answer for its work, is it deeper, is it truer, is it more revelatory of any personal vision of human life, such questions are unaskable in the least common denominator of talk; they require a subjective criterion which is not invokable collectively, the one criterion which is invokable is theatrical effectiveness, and all concepts of improvement in meeting it become involuntarily concepts of surrender to the customary diet of the behemoth.

Accordingly, the more the play is worked on, the less it reveals. But conversely, no individual can match the group play of intelligence, perception, and energy that the pooling of good minds focuses upon the objective task of building the immediacy of the show. It cannot be otherwise: the literary author creates in solitude for a reader in solitude; the collective mind laboring on the stage is in hand-in-glove congruence with the collective mind responding in the audience. The writer who laments it is "not his play" on the stage is an ungrateful egomaniac who should confine his work to the schizoid art of poetry; and I thought perhaps I would.

Fragments of these views rode with me as the train rattled on towards Hudson. In the last quarter-hour a flutter of fear overtook me that we had passed my destination, in more ways than one, and I would never get back to it; but a recognizable trackyard swam under the window, and the train slowed to a stop. When I descended the steps with my bags, I spied my wife's parents—she was home with our sick one-year-old—come to fetch me; out of their hands our other boy, looking strangely older in an unfamiliar and fierce deerslayer jacket, ran delightedly to meet me and I caught him up. I was out of the spaceship at last, back to earth, on solid ground where I belonged.

17

THAT night Leah worriedly phoned me to say that one of Fred's business representatives had worriedly phoned her to say that in his opinion the final scene of the play was not holding the audience and should be dropped from the show. I shuddered like a cracked bell under a sledgehammer. Such opinions were always around our ears like horseflies; agents, lawyers, their assistants, their assistants' secretaries, and their secretaries' husbands' secretaries, all bright heads, comprised a fourth species of co-workers who discharged the functions of the other three, advising us as impresarios, artists, and theatergoers; the one difficulty in implementing most of their recommendations was that they were time-consuming, costly, inappropriate, talentless, irresponsible, and mutually annihilative. I waited throughout the weekend for pressure to mount on the point, going into shell shock with each ring of the phone, but there was no word from Philadelphia. At midnight Saturday the company disbanded there, to reassemble at the theater in New York on Tuesday; the crew in the interim once more tore down, moved, and reunited the physical body of the show, while those in charge of its spirit rested on their first day off in almost nine weeks. When on Sunday evening I phoned Arthur at home—his voice sounded exhausted and shaky—he said all he wanted in the final scene was a few line cuts. Monday the entry in my notebook consisted of a single word, "Peace."

With Tuesday the final three-day hump in the roller-coaster ride hove in sight. After lunch I packed the station wagon, and drove my wife and four-year-old to New York. We all ran straight in the rain to the Booth Theatre: the set was up, with rehearsal in progress, and I saw at last we were in a house suited to the play, small, warm, intimate as a woman. Though most of the company were pleased to see us, and we them, the wheel was in motion and it was not from my family that I now felt the turn of estrangement.

In the evening we gave the first of two preview performances, for paying audiences; our all-or-nothing throw was to take place on Thursday. In the milling of the audience George Jenkins found occasion to tell my wife a tale of a playwright who had solved the difficulties of rewriting on the road by being carried away from a Boston hotel by men in white; I could well believe it. I thought the show that night not at all bad, though Fred and Arthur seemed harassed—I later learned there had been a twelve-inch misanticipation of backstage space, which among other ensnarlments resulted in Annie's being struck by one of the turntables moving in the dark—and the sense of closeness to the audience was heartening. It was a warm theater-party houseful, members of a Jewish organization, who watched with a special eye my Jewish urchin abandoned in the end by my Christian gentleman; and upon their exit one was overheard saying, "Well, what can you expect from a shegitz?" I went backstage to congratulate the actors, and found Hank already gone.

Arthur came in the morning to the apartment where we were staying, and we put in an hour or two cutting lines out of the third act, which cheered him up. I herded my wife and boy with me to the afternoon rehearsal—I was healing, but the new skin was thinly knit and in their presence I felt bandaged—where everyone returned my hello except Hank, who since I had locked up the typewriter was freezing me out. My boy was intrigued by the huge doll house of the set, and I wended with him up the spiral staircase to the grid overhanging the stage; while we peered down, Arthur, Annie, and Hank deep below stalled in an impasse over two or three lines, and presently Arthur was climbing to the grid after me, inescapable as Javert, and I altered the lines for him with my off-hand there. I attended the evening preview without bandages. This time I bore my congratulations backstage immediately, and said to Hank I had missed him the preceding night, he must have left the theater like a bat out of hell; he replied tersely, "Just as quick as I can." Fred and Arthur again seemed harassed, and to my weary disbelief—we were twenty hours away from our opening—requested a script conference. I had two friends at the preview, and I took them and Annie across the street for an ice-cream soda, and then walked to a theater-crowd restaurant where Fred and Arthur sat at a table awaiting me. Fred was gloomy, and Arthur was keyed up to a crisp efficiency; both of them wanted a transition in the penultimate scene made more explicit by added dialogue. My own impression was that further perfecting was more necessary to their internal dramas than to the one onstage, but I knew it was the last shred of rewriting I could be asked for—only because of time—and I said I would like not to discuss it, I would simply go back to our apartment and do it. I suspected it would not go into the show.

Nevertheless I sat up till three a.m. with the lines, slept until eight-thirty, worked on them in the morning for another two hours, and then calling Arthur, dictated the half page over the phone while he wrote it down. There was a silence, after which he said, "It seems enormous." I said it seemed so to me, I was opposed to its use, anything we gained in the dialogue we would lose by weakening the security of the performances, and I thought we were dumping our anxiety onto the actors. Arthur agreed, and said he would try that afternoon to achieve his point by directorial means instead. I thereupon took my boy for a pleasure trip in the subway—his idea of New York's outstanding tourist attraction—and spent the afternoon with him and his mother in a museum contemplating stars and dinosaur bones as a lesson in personal ambition. I also managed a late nap. Around six-thirty my wife and I dined with another couple at a restaurant in mid-town, where I was not uncalm but found a little food went a long way, and we walked to the theater. Our curtain was at eight o'clock.

It was a night I had taken aim at with a dream twenty years ago, but underneath some restiveness I was rather unimpressed: I had acquired a real life in the meantime, I knew where it was lived and with whom, and it was not alterable by any failure or success in 45th Street. The night was however a hectic one. I saw Fred on the sidewalk, handsome in evening attire and very pale; I asked how he was, and he said with a protectionless smile, "Weak." He was sitting on the lid of some information which would have distressed a number of us: the production was more than $14,000 in the red, and if it flopped that night an "overcall"—an assessment on backers for additional monies—would be necessary to pay our bills. My wife and I slipped in at the stage door to visit the actors in their make-up rooms. I wanted to say something not an empty compliment to Hank, and I found it; I said in view of how he felt I thought what he was doing was admirable, which elicited no reply, so I went downstairs to Annie and exchanged bulletins on the state of our thoraxes; I reported I was not anxious, only impatient, and Annie reported the same, she wanted to have at them and be done. The narrow spaces backstage, corridor and stairs, were growing crowded with well-wishers, in a cubbyhole of the mail rack two or three dozen telegrams had accumulated for me, and a fifth of bourbon with my name on it, whose donor I never identified, was put in my hand, which then carried it around for the rest of the evening. The theater was meanwhile filling with the audience, in lobby, aisles, and seat rows, a brilliant parade of evening finery and choice flesh, show-business celebrities (many of them familiar to me) and the cream of society (unfamiliar) and more than forty of my relatives and friends from four states (whose tickets I had made arrangements for and turned out now to be all in undesirable locations). I was making enemies right and left by spreading my greetings so thin each recipient felt especially slighted. My most eminent guest was my mother, a young woman of seventy, who had made a novena and been for months lighting holy-candles to Saint Anthony for the play's success; she had written me she had little doubt of it because it had "a good author, good actors, good director, and good prayers." At eight o'clock my wife and I joined her in the third row—there were no free seats, and even our pair cost us about seventeen dollars, to see a play I was somewhat acquainted with—next to my sister and brother-in-law, and with the back of my head vulnerable to the seven homicidal critics somewhere in the immediate vicinity behind it. There they sat, as usual, solely to appraise a bubble of a show, utterly ignorant of and unconcerned with the long fermentation of griefs it had risen out of, which was as it should be. Arthur and Fred were haunting the back aisle, and subsequently ducked out from time to time to fortify themselves spiritually across the street, a theater tradition I was violating in my seat, but I felt oddly content; we opened our first-night programs, a special edition with a golden cover, and read with interest therein the biographical summaries from which the five of us floated forth as darlings of the gods, airily leaping from success to success like pneumatic mountain goats; and the house-lights softly died, the audience grew still, and the stage-set swam into color out of the darkness.

The play happened brilliantly. Annie and Hank had never acted it better; they did nothing unrehearsed, that Arthur had not labored tirelessly for in the past ten weeks, but their best moments came together in one performance now, and I was reminded of a definition attributed to Jack Dempsey, a champion is someone who is at the peak of condition not five minutes before or after but at the precise instant the bell rings; for the first time in weeks I enjoyed the show. I thought it was worth seventeen dollars.

So it appeared did the audience, which meant little, since those of them who were not my relatives were someone else's; the critics rushed away to their newspaper offices to type out the truth. The next hour in the theater was like blossomtime in a beehive. I undertook to make friends by saying good-by to all the enemies I had made by saying hello, while the entire audience undertook to squeeze into the make-up rooms backstage; sometime in the midst thereof Arthur informed me over several heads that a radio review was already out and most enthusiastic. Our fate however lay with the newspaper reviews, and the company was to gather in a death watch for these in the apartment of Fred's agent. My wife and I eventually extricated ourselves via the stage door, and consulting a scrap of paper for the agent's address, put the theater behind us. We drifted on foot uptown with the crowd beneath the neon clamor of Broadway, a street we now either owned or were pariahs to; whichever, a wish that had begun almost five life-consuming years earlier, in a flickering image under my bald spot on a sleepless pillow, and come true in a peopled world of happenings too multiple to grasp or truly mirror herein, was done with. Midway to the agent's we hailed a cab and rode. In her apartment we found the beehive back in business, with all hands in attendance who bore any relation to the show, except Hank, together with their wives, in-laws, friends, foes, and hired neutrals in charge of tabled food and liquor. I became dreamy with gin as soon as I could. I passed the next hour or two not unpleasantly in a wandering hubbub of theater talk, while rumors of "raves" by the critics flew in and out; as Fred was called and recalled to the phone in the back bedroom, to listen to mysterious informants somewhere in the night world of the city, my wife and I settled in there to overhear; and at last we had two reviews verbatim, which Fred phoned to Hank at his home, Atkinson favorable, Kerr less so, and neither to my ears a rave. I then escorted my wife and fifth of bourbon in a taxi back to our apartment foreseeing our reception as mixed and tepid, and a bit depressed that I was not the writer I wanted to be, but that was all right too, and sometime around three o'clock my wife and I were in bed together, asleep.

I awoke into our seventy-fifth day before noon, dressed, ate breakfast, went out to a corner newsstand and bought all the papers, came back with them, phoned Arthur, phoned Fred, packed my wife and boy into the station wagon, and by one o'clock was driving them homewards in the queer knowledge that the family now included a behemoth made of solid gold.

18

BROOKS ATKINSON'S review in *The New York Times* was headed "Fonda, Anne Bancroft in Play at Booth":

Although William Gibson has only two characters in "Two for the Seesaw" he has a tender style of writing and a beautiful little story to tell. And in the production that opened at the Booth last evening, he has two extraordinarily winning actors.

Everyone knows one of them. Henry Fonda is on one end of the seesaw, playing the part of the man who is out of love with his wife in Omaha, and not sure that he is in love with a girl in New York who has worldly ideas. Mr. Fonda is a wonderfully straightforward actor who plays at low pressure. As Jerry in Mr. Gibson's play, he gives his most limpid and moving performance. What he does not say in the dialogue, he says with the silent eloquence of a fine actor.

Anne Bancroft is on the other end of the seesaw—an attractive young actress unknown to this department until last evening, but sure to be known to thousands of theatregoers before the season is over. She plays the part of Gittel, a rather ordinary New York semi-bohemian. She lives alone. She tries to believe that she is a ballet dancer. She is full of schemes and projects, none of which is worth a dime. Goodhearted, unselfish, she unwittingly lives for other people.

The part is extremely well-written in the vernacular, though never cheap or mannered. Mr. Gibson has given her a great many comic and touching things to say. But if Miss Bancroft were not a glowing young lady without a mean bone in her body, the dialogue might sound more clever than honest. She is the animated half of the cast, making a vivid contrast with Mr. Fonda's leisurely style; she explodes with gestures that are natural; she modulates the part with vocal inflections that are both funny and authentic, and she creates a gallant character who rings true.

When the curtain goes up, "Two for the Seesaw" looks like a plausible stunt. A man in a shabby room in one corner of New York is telephoning to a girl who lives in a cheap apartment decorated with a dressmaker's form and earnest art objects. In the first scene we seem to be promised one more whirl at the epic theme of two unattached people in New York. This situation has already provided us with a whole library of tasteless, squalid, prurient comedies.

But Mr. Gibson is a genuine writer. No doubt he uses the two-character form cleverly. But it is not long before "Two for the Seesaw" turns out to be a fresh and amusing comedy that is really interested in the characters of two decent people. The talk is funny; the habits of the two characters are breezy. But Jerry has standards, and so has Gittel. They learn some illuminating truths about themselves from each other. By the time the curtain comes down, you are not so much aware that Mr. Gibson has brought off a technical stunt as that he has looked inside the hearts of two admirable people and made a charming full-length play out of them.

Everyone concerned with this miniature triumph has contributed his own kind of distinction. Arthur Penn's unobtrusive direction gets over the technical hurdles easily and goes on to help develop and analyze the characters. George Jenkins' warm and pleasant settings, against a towering skyline, bring variety into the play and help to explain the moral experience of the two people who inhabit them.

For "Two for the Seesaw" is a finely wrought cameo. Thanks to Mr. Gibson's thoughtful writing and to the soft, shining acting by Mr. Fonda and Miss Bancroft, it has style, beauty, and a delightful point of view.

Walter Kerr's review in the New York *Herald Tribune* was headed "Two for the Seesaw":

At the end of the second act of "Two for the Seesaw," Anne Bancroft huddles herself in a ratty seal jacket, shakes the unkempt hair out of her face long enough to rasp out a sassy, bitter defense of her two buck teeth, spills a cup of hot milk all over her unsteady chin, then doubles her black-stockinged feet under her to rock back and forth in ulcerous pain—while Henry Fonda looks on and tells her she's beautiful.

The odd thing about it is that he's quite right. Miss Bancroft, hoisting one side of her mouth to let rip with a fine old Bronx phrase or flinging one helpless hand halfway into the air like a cheerless Girl Scout who never got to camp, radiates a wild and wilful and wonderfully funny integrity that makes a couple of shabby tenement rooms look as though they were lighted by chandeliers.

The young actress, who seems to have just come to us from television, has the kind of natural, offhand, nobody-asked-me warmth that turns red-hot gas grates chilly by comparison. She treats a telephone with the contempt normally reserved for an intimate member of the family. ("Sophie, don't be a friend—be an enemy, and don't pester me.") She falls over a dressmaker's dummy with the awkward and clattering splendor of a twelve-year-old. She mourns over the French-fries she can't eat with the deathbed ardor of a Camille, and she turns a phrase like "ye gods" into a purring sound of ecstatic approval.

But Miss Bancroft has something more than the tart, shoulder-shrugging, know-it-all innocence of the patsy she is playing at the Booth. She has, in addition, the range of one of the newer guided missiles. William Gibson's two-character exercise may ask her, after George Jenkins' very flexible scenery has transported her to another disordered room, to shift gears from the bright, curt, cryptically tangled nonsense of a bantering exchange with Henry Fonda to the dour and nearly desperate melodrama of carefully concealing an illness from a man she is afraid she is going to lose. The girl slips, almost without our noticing it, into the grim and touching second tone—and makes it stick. We have been handed, gratis, a brand new, first-rate performer.

There is a second name connected with "Two for the Seesaw" you'll want to keep your eye on, though perhaps more for promise than for absolute performance this time out. Author William Gibson has a deft, buoyant, rapid-fire flair for dialogue, he is perfectly able to keep an evening moving in spite of all the telephoning, and his eye for accurately observed detail is excellent.

What he hasn't quite mastered at the moment—and this seriously involves the earnest and accomplished Mr. Fonda —is the business of sustaining a psychology, a troubled and uncertain state of mind, through all its possible dramatic complexities. Henry Fonda meets Miss Bancroft while he is in the process of divorcing his wife. He has, he tells us, been accepting emotional and financial "handouts" all his life; it is time he helped someone else. Thereafter he is torn between Miss Bancroft, who does need his help, and the wife whose spiritual presence he cannot shake.

The seesaw rides up and down. But the force of gravity which brings it earthward each time is never powerfully felt. The wife seems an unidentified convention, Mr. Fonda's concern is for a very long time inexplicable, and the trivial jealousies that beset our onstage couple stem from sources that seem small, insubstantial, and a shade self-pitying. The tools are in excellent shape; the hand that wields them is not quite firm.

John Chapman's review in the *New York Daily News* was headed " 'Two for Seesaw' Captivating":

The rarest and most difficult venture in the theatre is a two-character play. It was difficult, at any rate, up to last evening, when a romantic comedy by William Gibson, "Two for the Seesaw," was presented at the Booth Theatre. Gibson has made such a tricky task look as easy as pie. At the Booth, two's company, and the play is an absorbing, affectionate and funny delight.

The author has had plenty of help, of course. He has had the good fortune to have Henry Fonda and Anne Bancroft. We all know about Fonda, for he is an old pro. All we know about Miss Bancroft is that she is new to the Broadway stage and a perfect treasure. Here is a comedienne, reared in TV and a couple of movies, who has the gift of doing precisely the right thing at every moment. Her timing of movement and speech are flawless, and her warmth of personality is more than considerable.

There is further help at hand for author Gibson, who also is new to the theatre. Another old pro, George Jenkins, has devised a pair of one-room Manhattan apartments which are constantly on the move—thanks, no doubt, to a dozen or so unseen stagehands. Another new pro, also a TV trainee, has directed the comedy with a great eye for pantomime as well as pace. His name is Arthur Penn. The producer, Fred Coe, also is making his Broadway bow, but his picture-tube reputation is considerable. Give Coe credit for taking a big risk on a very small play.

The plot is a simple one about a man and a girl, each living alone, who get together through a chance telephone call. No more of the details should be told, for the telling is best done by Miss Bancroft and Fonda. She is a New York-bred Jewish girl, both wise and innocent for her years, and he is a Nebraskan on the lam from an estranged wife. The ending is not the sugary affair one might expect, but it is both intelligent and right.

It's a long play, too—nine scenes, but when it was over

last evening I wondered how and where the time had flown. "Two for the Seesaw" could have been a hollow artifice, but instead it is an adult and charming work. An adult eastern, indeed.

Robert Coleman's review in the *New York Mirror* was headed " 'Two for the Seesaw' a Hit":

"Two for the Seesaw," a "sleeper" if we ever caught one, teetered into the Booth Theatre Thursday evening for what promises to be a lengthy stay. When word got around that the new entry had but two in its cast, we were, as Smith and Dale would put it, dubious.

For the toughest thing we know is to fill an evening in a show-shop with a mere duo on stage. After all, the late John Van Druten had to use a trio to keep his "Voice of the Turtle" packing the customers in. And you'd be surprised how handy that extra character can be.

He or she obviates a lot of telephone calls and talks with off-set people who are never seen. Well, William Gibson employs Alexander Graham Bell's invention often, in this instance. But it seems as natural as a snowstorm in winter, and pushes the action forward. It never obtrudes as an artificial device to pad out scenes.

"Two for the Seesaw" has to do with a lawyer from Nebraska, who comes to New York to discover if he could stand on his own feet. His doting wife and influential father-in-law have made success too easy for him. He meets Gittel Mosca, an ambitious dancer with an ulcer, who has grown up in the school of hard knocks.

She gets the idea that he might marry her after his spouse divorces him. But their environments have been so different that it's just not in the cards. They learn a lot from each other, and he eventually goes home when his wife needs him. Now he can do things for her instead of always having them done for him.

That's a simple story, but it's packed with humanity and humor. Gibson knows what makes people tick, and how to project it. He has a flair for speech that is accurate and flavorsome. And, like Bill Saroyan, he loves people, though he sees them realistically, rather than through rose-tinted glasses.

Fred Coe is a remarkable man. Over the years, he has developed a stable of young writers via TV, who are making important contributions to the theatre. He also has encouraged young players and directors. Now it looks as though the bread he's been casting on the waters is going to return to him as golden loaves.

It was sheer inspiration that prompted Coe to sign Anne Bancroft to make her Broadway bow opposite Henry Fonda in "Two for the Seesaw." She is the perfect Gittel Mosca, a tough little cookie with a big heart. She's been kicked around, craves affection, and knows how to bestow it.

With touseled black hair, a slouching walk, saucer-like eyes and a mouth that matches her hands in expressiveness, she is the most engaging gamine to light up a stage in many a semester. She completely captivated the first-nighters at the Booth, who were happy to sit in at the birth of a new star.

As for Fonda, he set up the laughs, for Miss Bancroft to cash in on, with superlative skill. And, in his unshowy way, etched a winningly honest portrait of a troubled man in search of his soul. That Fonda and Miss Bancroft held an audience spellbound for more than two and a half hours was a feat nothing short of miraculous.

Arthur Penn, making his directorial debut on the Main Stem, has staged Gibson's bombshell of emotion and hilarity magnificently. You'd better rush to the Booth boxoffice immediately if you expect to obtain two for "The Seesaw" in the foreseeable future. It's a whale of a hit, a bittersweet joy ride.

Frank Aston's review in the *New York World-Telegram* was headed "Play Has Cast For Two Only":

The novelty of "Two for the Seesaw" is, of course, the demonstration that two persons, and two only, can populate a stage and keep things going through nine scenes of three acts. This trick, last done on Broadway by Hume Cronyn and Jessica Tandy, is being accomplished at the Booth by Henry Fonda and Anne Bancroft, operating in a Jenkins setting which moves your attention smoothly around two murky flats. Both players are highly gifted. In fact, the playing is the endeavor's chief hope of survival.

The lanky Fonda, secure with dry delivery and understated emphasis, could grip any audience on which he might concentrate. In the current instance, he is concentrating for dear life.

Miss Bancroft, new to the New York stage, turns out to be a deliriously captivating comic, a rich discovery, a youngster who should do much for the W. 40s. At the Booth she is strictly Bronx, inflection, grimace, shrug, and all. She can make big ones out of minor ones like, "You know what you got too much of? Lack of self-confidence." And she's pretty enough to make you overlook such gems as, "So this is health bread? What'd they do, cut it right off the stump?"

Their story concerns a Midwestern lawyer, wretched and alone in New York, waiting for his wife to get a divorce back home. He wanders into a stormy love affair with a volatile dummy, who also lives alone, but doesn't starve for male company. As they seesaw through a winter, she encourages him to try the law again. At first she is doing everything for him. He moodily plugs toward modest success in an attorney's office, while growing more and more neurotic. The girl comes down with duodenal hemorrhages, and then it seems he is doing everything for her. They make torrid love, cussing and quarreling the while. And the question that finally must be answered is: Does he truly love this gamin or his wife, who, though unseen, sounds batty herself.

To this spectator neither character attained any measure of reality. They were no more than amusing, as when Mr. Fonda playing straight man, grinned at Miss Bancroft's: "For supper I got a bargain. Wine! Only 69 cents a bottle. It was getting old, I guess?"

Funny gal. But the play could be better.

John McClain's review in the *New York Journal American* was headed "Fabulous Freak a Hit":

The proceedings at the Booth last night, the opening of a new play called "Two for the Seesaw," provided the season with a fabulous freak. For here we have an excellent drama, a runaway hit, involving the services of just five people—a producer, a writer, two actors and a director. The sets are simple, the costumes are plain and practical. It all seems ridiculously easy.

But of course it isn't, and for this the burden of praise must go to the author, a first-timer named William Gibson. He tells a poignant and plausible story of the regeneration of two lost souls, a mid-Western lawyer and a girl from the Bronx.

They are thrown together in the solitude of Manhattan, they cling to one another, and from this warmth and understanding comes the promise of a new life.

Mr. Gibson has two enormous talents going for him: a wild and beautiful sense of humor and a meticulous ear. His girl is the most authentic and hilarious exponent of Bronx-American since the early Goldbergs, and his boy is a serious and dimensional study of enlightened Nebraska.

The basic conflicts of the play ebb and flow at times, but the emotional values are intact. We are captured by these two people, their problems become ours.

The author has constructed his story well. The first act is most difficult, for it never reveals the reasons for the boy's odd behavior. This, of course, opens the second act wide and takes him happily through the dead middle, to which so many plays fall victim. The third act offers a moving and credible conclusion. Mr. Gibson can really write.

Henry Fonda has never given a poor performance within my memory, but this may be one of his best.

The role of a disillusioned attorney, his marriage a failure as he faces loneliness and desolation, is hand-tailored to his talents. It is, of course, an exhaustive part and he takes full advantage of even the most minute pantomime. (He has to: he's never off the stage for more than a minute.)

As the girl, Anne Bancroft makes her Broadway bow, and threatens at times to take the entire theatre under her arm and go home. Her accent, the gesture with the cupped left hand, are as native to her neighborhood as gefüllte fish.

She can swear outlandishly without being at all vulgar; in the next sentence she can break your heart. I would call her an exceptional young actress.

This is one play about which it can be said with some assurance that the direction is outstanding. With only two people it has to be, to remain unobtrusive, and for this credit Arthur Penn, also a Broadway newcomer.

Any two-character play runs the risk of emerging as a trick, or a bit of show-off. "Seesaw" has none of that feeling; there are no times when anybody else is needed, or wanted. It is thoroughly delightful and compelling theatre, and I know where Mr. Fonda can get a nice apartment. The owner wants a two-year lease, but Mr. Fonda shouldn't mind that.

Richard Watts' review in the *New York Post** was headed "Striking Play With Two Players":

A play with only two characters, however expert it may be, almost inevitably takes on the quality of a theatrical stunt, and it is one of the outstanding merits of William Gibson's "Two for the Seesaw," which opened last night at the Booth, that it is so much more than bright trickery. The deft humor and the atmosphere of romantic comedy are there, but they are underlined by an unexpected kind of sad and rueful honesty that lifts the narrative beyond mechanical sprightliness and gives it an admirable feeling of poignant dramatic truth.

The pair of players who carry the entire burden of the evening on their shoulders have an enormous responsibility, and here "Two for the Seesaw" is especially happy. Being an experienced actor of quiet skill and complete credibility, Henry Fonda is naturally excellent in his share of the proceedings, but the exhilarating surprise is that a young actress from the films named Anne Bancroft, who is making her first Broadway appearance, gives so brilliant a performance opposite him that Mr. Fonda is pushed to keep from seeming almost her straight man.

The story is of a young attorney from Nebraska, lost, alone and unhappy in New York and about to be divorced by the wife he loves, and of his encounter with a courageous but upset and defeated girl dancer from the Bronx. There is the expected romantic attachment between them, and the romance, although depicted with unusual sympathy and understanding, seems destined for the customary path of the fabricated theatrical love story. The author, however, is concerned with truth, and instead of the obvious, he gives us something moving and inexorable.

It is in the nature of the two-character play that it occasionally seems on the verge of straining to keep going and of relying rather desperately on the intervention of the telephone. But Mr. Gibson always has the skill to save himself in time, at first by the deftness of his characterization and a striking ability to write lines that are freshly and genuinely humorous and real, and, finally, by his determination to avoid mere attractive fabrication and follow his narrative to its logical and even upsetting conclusion.

It is clear that this new dramatist is both an expert craftsman and an honest and compassionate observer, with an engaging sense of humor. He can write fine roles for actors able to take advantage of them, and it is pleasant to find that his players live up to their opportunities. Nothing could be much more enchanting than Miss Bancroft's portrayal of the Bronx girl. She has humor, fire, emotional power, depth, insight and variety, and her performance is not only moving and charming but reveals a sensitive intelligence of high distinction.

Mr. Fonda's role is basically less interesting, but he plays it with that apparently casual deftness of his which makes even the weaker aspects of the lawyer's character real and oddly appealing. Arthur Penn's direction is admirable, giving the play the required showmanship without sacrificing its integrity, and George Jenkins' settings capture its mood perfectly and ingeniously. With Mr. Gibson's sympathetic skill as a dramatist, combined with the notable playing of Mr. Fonda and Miss Bancroft, "Two for the Seesaw" is one of the season's blessings.

19

MUCH remains to be told, but none of it in this account, except for curtain calls.

In the days that followed the reviews multiplied fast, in trade periodicals, out-of-town newspapers, weekly and monthly magazines; it transpired our show was not only a hit, but a smash hit, lo, one of the smash hits of the generation. Though we spent a minimum on advertising, word of mouth was so infectious—our salaried ears in the lobby reported they never heard a word of adverse criticism—that the line of ticket buyers snaked out of the theater down the street, Fred put on extra hands at the box office, the theater management broke through the wall to install another ticket window, and weeks later I saw in a newspaper the show had set a new record for attendance in the Booth's forty-five-year history. In the fifth week there, our statement of operations read, typically enough, thus:

BOX OFFICE RECEIPTS	$31,898.77	
Less: Theater share	7,974.69	
Company share	$23,924.08	
Insurance claim	—	(2nd week: $6,000.00)
Advertising allowance (by theater)	500.00	
TOTAL INCOME	$24,424.08	
EXPENSES		
Salaries:		
Cast	$ 5,446.84	
Stage managers	550.00	
Company manager	350.00	
Press agent	260.00	
Crew	1,825.00	
Wardrobe and dressers	195.00	
Stagehands	263.30	

Royalties:		
Author	2,889.88	
Director	797.47	
Publicity		
Share of newspapers	878.25	
Photos and signs	—	(3rd week: $633.60)
Printing and promotion	500.00	
Press expense	69.75	
Department:		
Stage manager	—	(1st week: $50.91)
Electrical	17.61	
Property	60.84	
Wardrobe	148.51	
Carpenter	—	(4th week: $113.08)
Rentals—electrical and sound equipment	386.48	
Railroad	—	(1st week: $248.09)
Box office	275.62	
Transfer and cartage	—	(1st week: $3,504.68)
Office expense	250.00	
Auditing	60.00	
Payroll taxes	219.05	
Insurance	322.94	
General business tax	59.81	
Medical expense	—	(2nd week: $150.00)
TOTAL EXPENSES	$15,826.35	
OPERATING PROFIT	$ 8,597.73	

Negotiations throughout the spring ended in contracts for the "national company"—two other actors who would be sent on tour with the play to a dozen major cities—and for productions abroad in England, Scandinavia, Holland, France, Germany, Italy, Mexico, Greece, Puerto Rico, Australia, Argentina, South Africa; this small play had become a large international industry, and Mars seemed more imminent. In June, Fred and I sat together in Leah's office for the first time since our initial meeting there, almost two years before, when my hopes were up that he would take the script under option for $200 a month; we were now present to sign a seventy-five-page contract it had taken Leah and Fred's lawyer months of brilliant maneuvering to conclude, selling the play to the movies for $600,000 and a percentage of the gross. One of the other agents hovering over the show estimated that its total profits, accruing to all participants over the years, would be conservatively in the neighborhood of two million dollars, the bulk of it going alas to the tax collector.

It was a better neighborhood than I foresaw when I gave my first readings of the play to lukewarm listeners and concluded I had wasted a year in writing a dud. The script and all of us had traveled a long row under the harrow since then. It would be impossible to assay how much of whom was in this greenback crop; patently it was no accident, it was made, and it was made in this show alone of all the shows we met on the road. Certainly it was unthinkable without first and foremost Arthur, who not only put his rare intelligence at the service of the writing long before we had a producer, but himself found the producer, gave a rigorous script a stage life of maximal variety and inventiveness, comedic, intense, humane, and in our direst period had the agile wit to outline most of the workable play needed to mediate between my play and Hank's; or without Hank, whose word to "start it rolling" caused the entire production to materialize, and who by his indestructible honesty onstage won the audience to the most unwinning moments in my man; or without Fred, who with the tenacity of a snapping turtle let go of no item under his eye in any department, including the script, until it was as close to perfection as mortal flesh could carry it; or without

Annie, who made of one role the key to unlock a lifetime of talent in a characterization every detail of which rang alive with the unmatchable authority of a unique artist.

It would be pleasant to end on the note that with our efforts thus crowned by monetary success, and an incessant buzz of praise instead of horseflies around our ears, the pleasures of fame and fortune made all our sufferings worthwhile, and we lived happily thereafter. The truth was more original.

Three days after we opened Hank fell prey to the flu and was out of the show for a week; he would have no part of the praise—or so I heard at second hand, respecting his wish that I not visit his make-up room—and the half year until his contract released him saw no dilution of his dissatisfaction. Annie, who had so put Broadway in her purse on opening night that her interviews had to be rationed, sounded only depleted when I phoned her soon after; she said she was "too tired to be anything but sweet." Arthur in a rehearsal after Hank's illness came upon scenes so disturbing and redintegrative of anxieties he had to skip over them, and Fred in a visit to the show five months later was still unable to watch certain passages without "breaking out in a cold sweat" of memory. I holed up in the bosom of my family in so violent a distaste for matter theatric that when I gazed at talent on our TV screen my teeth went into a chatter; I saw the play only once in its next six months. For none of us was this success an occasion for jubilation: it seemed prevalently one of weariness, bewilderment, even loss.

I had experienced success before, and been nourished by it. What I had never experienced was one that felt so much like failure; to me there was something destructive in such success, a few more victories like this and I was lost. I was ungratified by the compliments on the writing, as though I had won a beauty contest by appearing in a falseface, much improved by Arthur's ears and Fred's nose, a rich thing but not mine own. I suspected that this was merely the sulks, until it was time to deliver the text to my publisher; reading it over then I saw that what was spoken on the stage might serve it well enough, but I could not put my name to it in cold print. I spent two weeks in revising it for the last time, retaining many of the lines we had arrived at, but restoring much of what I had surrendered, and writing new bits as well. It is this composite of several versions which appears in the pages following. And when in its subsequent productions I found it still impossible for valid box-office reasons to push through the casting I really wanted, my opinion acquired a fixative: one might say many enthusiastic and truthful things about the rewards of the professional theater, such as the money, and the comradeship, and the money, and the self-espials, and the money, but to me they all lay in the arms of the truth that the theater, in this country, in this decade, was primarily a place not in which to be serious, but in which to be likeable; and it behooved each of us in it to do careful bookkeeping on his soul, lest it grow, like the dyer's hand, subdued to what it works in.

20

So I pastured my soul in the Berkshire hills and the solitary prose of this log, doing my bookkeeping, in an effort to make some sense out of a major piece of confusion in my life. Its purpose thus grew in the writing: it was no longer a refuge or a salvage, but a seeking.

It was written with unease, in leisure provided by the very success it does penance for. Human action is replete with misjudgments and false starts, small ambitions, stratagems for survival, all the imperfections of our nature, one of the kindliest being the gift to misremember or forget them. To impale them so on the wing was not altogether agreeable to me or just to any of us. Yet it was precisely out of such failings, with hard labor, that our success was made; that seemed worth saying. Success is an analgesic and an opiate, and to let it deaden in memory the unhappy stuff of which it is born was to me a loss quite analagous to the one I felt in my own work; it was poorer without its blemishes, some of which were founded deeper and prized by me more than its impeccabilities. Yet others might think otherwise, and neither in the production nor in this fractional history of it was the material solely mine. I allayed my misgivings in part by sending the completed log to my collaborators, and modifying it on request.

I worked in it toward an understanding. It is why we tell any history, and make such art as plays. History mirrors some facts of the outer and infinite world, compared to which the fictions we invent in art are flimsy stereotypes; but it is never self-contained, and one ignored fact can crack the mirror; there is no last word. Art is history of an interior kind, whose cardinal tenet is wholeness; it woos wholeness by setting its limits, and within them loosing truth against contrary truth in a struggle to a quietude which embraces and reconciles both; to whatever degree it achieves this, its matter lies beyond debate. It seems to me no piece of writing is worth its ink unless it thus marries contrarieties and has issue; to relive the events herein would be an unaffordable luxury of pain if I thought it without some offspring of truth. Yet it is only mine, and every pattern of meaning lifted from the welter of the world is simultaneously a discovery and a lie. It is no reason to be mute: we could do with more, but not less.

I have in this history imitated some of the structure of art. It is no disguise for the fact that it is a one-eyed history; it leaves much to be debated; and its last word can be only that it is a relief now to have done with facts, and let fiction speak for itself.

TWO *for the* SEESAW

WILLIAM GIBSON

Characters

JERRY RYAN
GITTEL MOSCA

THE ACTION takes place this past year, between fall and spring, in two rooms—Jerry's and Gittel's—in New York City.

ACT ONE:	*Scene I*	Both rooms. September, late afternoon.
	Scene II	Gittel's room. Midnight, the same day.
	Scene III	Both rooms. Daybreak following.
ACT TWO:	*Scene I*	Jerry's room. October, dusk.
	Scene II	Both rooms. December, noon.
	Scene III	Gittel's room. February, a Saturday night.
ACT THREE:	*Scene I*	Gittel's room. March, midday.
	Scene II	Jerry's room. May, dusk.
	Scene III	Both rooms. A few days later, afternoon.

THE SET consists of two rooms, angled toward each other, but in no way related; they are in different buildings, a few miles apart, in New York.

THE ROOM ON STAGE RIGHT is Jerry Ryan's and is the tiny living-room of a bleak two-room flat in a lower East Side tenement. It contains principally a narrow couch with a kitchen chair at its side, and at the beginning has the depressing air of having been moved into recently and minimally; the telephone for instance sits on the bare floor. In the right wall is a window through which we see nearby rooftops. In the rear wall is a doorway which opens into a kitchen so dark it is practically indecipherable; in this kitchen is a gas range, a covered bathtub, and the entrance door of the flat. The left wall of the room towards stage center is omitted or fragmented, so as not to obstruct our view of the other room on the stage.

THE ROOM ON STAGE LEFT is Gittel Mosca's and is the living-room of a flat in a run-down brownstone in midtown. It is on a lower level than Jerry's, is larger and lighter, and has a pleasantly untidy and cluttered air of having been lived in for some time; though furnished in very ordinary taste, it speaks of human comfort and warmth. Downstage in the left wall is the entrance door, and upstage a doorway into the kitchen, which is partly visible. The room contains among other things a studio double bed, a night table with lamp and phone, a bureau, chairs, and a dress dummy and sewing machine in the corner; there is also a window which looks out upon the street.

ACT ONE

Scene 1

BOTH ROOMS. IT IS A LATE AFTERNOON IN SEPTEMBER; THE WINDOWS OF BOTH ROOMS ARE OPEN, AND THE SOUNDS OF TRAFFIC FLOAT IN.

GITTEL'S *room is empty.*

In the other room JERRY *is sitting on his couch, cigarette in hand, searching with his finger down the phone book open between his feet.* JERRY *is a long fellow in his thirties, attractive, with an underlayer of melancholy and, deeper, a lurking anger; his manner of dress, which is casually conservative, is too prosperous for this drab and disorderly room. The couch is unmade, the kitchen chair next to it has a typewriter on it and is hung with clothes, a handsome suitcase is open on the unswept floor, and the dust is gathering in bunches along the baseboard. Now* JERRY *finds the number he wants, and dials.*

The phone in GITTEL's *room rings.*

On the fourth ring JERRY *hangs up. Simultaneously there has been a rattle of key and knob at* GITTEL's *door; she runs in, not stopping to set down her bag of groceries, and grabs the phone.*

GITTEL [OUT OF BREATH] Yeah, hello?

(*She waits a second.*)

Oh, hell.

(*She hangs up. She is a dark, thin girl of indeterminate age, too eccentric to be called pretty, nervous, uncouth, and engaging by virtue of some indestructible cheerfulness in her; all her clothes—denim skirt, peasant blouse, sandals—are somehow misfits, and everything she does has the jerky and lightweight intensity of a bird on the ground.*

Now she and JERRY *go about their separate business.*

JERRY *lifts the suitcase onto the couch, and taking out his clothes—a fine jacket, a fine suit, a fine topcoat—begins hanging them on a clothes rod set catty-corner between two walls; while he is putting some shoes down, the rod slips out of one support and everything falls on his head.*)

JERRY Oh, you son of a bitch.

(*He lets it all lie, and returns into the kitchen. He comes back with a block of wood, hammer, and nails; he nails the block any which way under the socket on one wall, puts the rod back in place, and hangs the clothes up again; this time the rod holds.*

Meanwhile GITTEL, *on her way to the kitchen with her bag of groceries, has stopped in front of the dress dummy and looks critically at a gaudy bodice pinned together on it; she stands unmoving for a minute, then with her free hand unpins the collar and commences to work. After a while she steps back, and is disgusted.*)

GITTEL Oh, for Christ sakes.

(*She gives up, slaps the pins down, and continues on to the kitchen, where we see her pour out a panful of milk and set it to warm on a gas burner; she puts the other groceries away in cupboard and icebox.* JERRY *finishes with his clothes, turns to regard the phone, sits on the couch, checks the same number, and dials it once more. The phone in* GITTEL'S *room rings.* GITTEL *runs back and answers it just as* JERRY *is about to hang up after two rings.*)

Yeah, hello?

(JERRY'S *voice when we hear it now is well-educated, with a deadpan mockery in it that is essentially detached.*)

JERRY Gittel Mosca, please.

GITTEL It's me, who's this?

JERRY This is Jerry Ryan. We met across eight or nine unidentified bodies last night at Oscar's. I'm a slight acquaintance of his from back home.

GITTEL Oh?

JERRY I say slight, about 170 pounds. Six one.

(*Waits; then elaborately:*)

Red beard—

GITTEL Oh, you were the fella in the dark hat that didn't say anything!

JERRY You must know some very bright hats. I overheard you talk about a frigidaire you want to sell. Be all right if I stop by for a look?

GITTEL At that frigidaire?

JERRY It's all I had in mind, to begin with.

GITTEL It's not a frigidaire, it's an icebox.

JERRY Good enough. No electric bill, a product of American know-how. I could be there in about—

GITTEL I gave it away!

JERRY [A PAUSE, STYMIED] Oh. Not very kind of you.

GITTEL I just helped him lug it home. Some jerk I never saw in my life, Sophie sent him over, so I let him have it just to get rid of the goddam thing. Why didn't you ask me last night?

JERRY I didn't want to be among the quick. Last night.

GITTEL Huh?

JERRY I changed my mind and life today, great day, I thought I'd start by putting my nose in on you for a look.

GITTEL It just isn't here.

JERRY So you said.

(*A pause, both waiting*)

Yes. Thanks anyway.

GITTEL Sure.

(JERRY *hangs up.*)

Oh, hell.

(*She hangs up too.* JERRY *after a morose moment gets up, fingers in his pack of cigarettes, finds it empty. En route to the window with it he bumps his knee against the couch; he lifts his foot and shoves it back, it jars the wall, the clothes rod is jogged out of the other support, and the clothes fall on the floor.*)

JERRY Agh, you son of a bitch!

(*He grabs the rod and brings it down over his knee; it only bends, flies up in his face. He attacks it again, can't break it, trips over it, and doesn't know where to get rid of it, in a rage which is comic, until suddenly he throws a short punch into the window, not comic; the glass flies. He stands, grimly considers his fist, his surroundings, his state of mind, gets away from the window, walks into the phone on the floor, regards it, gathers it up, and dials. Meanwhile* GITTEL'S *milk boils over as she is removing her sandals. She jumps up, and is hurrying toward the kitchen when her phone rings.*)

GITTEL Oh, for Christ sakes.

(*She is undecided, then hurries back and grabs up the phone.*)

Just a minute, will you, I'm boiling over.

(*She lays it down, hurries into the kitchen, turns the milk off, and comes back to the phone.*)

Milk all over the goddam stove, yeah?

(JERRY *sits with his eyes closed, the mouthpiece against his eyebrows.*)

Hello?

(JERRY *separates his face and the mouthpiece.*)

Hello, is anybody on this line?

JERRY No.

GITTEL Huh?

(JERRY *hangs up.*)

Hey!

(*She stares at the phone in her hand, then replaces it. She decides to shrug it off and go back to her milk, which she cools off by adding more from the container; but she stands in the doorway sipping it for only a second, then makes for the phone. She dials, and waits.* JERRY *walking in his room finds his hand is bleeding a bit, wraps it in his handkerchief, and has a private argument, not liking himself.*)

JERRY You brokenhearted fly, *begin.*

(*He gazes around the bare room, answers himself mordantly.*)

Begin what? The conquest of the Sunday *Times?*

(*He shoves the suitcase off the couch, lies down and extracts section after section of newspaper from under him, flinging them away.* GITTEL *gets an answer.*)

GITTEL Sophie. Is Oscar there? . . . Well, listen, that hat-type friend of his last night, the long one, what's his number? . . . Look, girl, will you drag your mind up out of your girdle and go see if Oscar's got it written down?

(JERRY'S *legs are overhanging, he moves back, but now his head bumps the wall. He gets to his feet and considers the couch grimly, muttering:*)

JERRY Six feet of man, five feet of couch, calls for a new man.

(*He stands the suitcase on end at the couch foot, lies down again with his feet out upon it, and extracts and flings away a final section of newspaper.* GITTEL *scribbles.*)

GITTEL 69 what? Yeah, yeah, yeah, very funny.

(*She clicks down, and immediately dials it.* JERRY'S *phone rings. His head lifts to regard it, and he lets it ring another time before he leans over to pick it up.*)

JERRY [GUARDEDLY] Yes?

GITTEL [QUICKLY, A LITTLE NERVOUS] Look, I been thinking here about that icebox, what we could do is I could take you around the corner where this character lives, if you offer him a buck or two he might turn loose of it, and it's worth five easy, what do you say?

(JERRY *on his elbow mulls her over.*)

Hey, you still with me?

JERRY I don't know yet, I might be against you. I'm not in the book, how did you get my number?

GITTEL Sophie gave me it. Now about this icebox, I mean for nothing I let this kid have a real bargain, you could afford to make it worth his while, what do you think?

JERRY I think you can't be calling about an icebox you had to help someone carry through the streets to get rid of.

GITTEL What do you mean?

JERRY You're calling either because like me you have nothing better to do, or because you're under the misap—

GITTEL [INDIGNANTLY] I got eleven different things I could be doing!

JERRY Different isn't better, why aren't we doing them? Or because you're under the misapprehension it was me who just hung up on you.

GITTEL [CONFUSED] Uh—it wasn't?

JERRY Whoever it was had a reason. Question now is what's yours? If a man calls up to say he's not calling up, a girl who calls him back can be either lonely, solicitous, prying, a help or a nuisance—

GITTEL Look, how'd I get in the wrong here?

JERRY —and I'm curious to know which.

GITTEL Did you call me up about this icebox or not?

JERRY Not.

(GITTEL *bangs the phone down, gets up, and tears her scrap of paper with his number into bits; she throws them into the wastebasket.* JERRY *after a surprised moment finds this somewhat amusing, smiles in spite of himself, clicks down, and dials back.* GITTEL'S *phone rings, and she comes to answer it;* JERRY'S *manner now is rather teasing.*)

GITTEL Yeah, hello?

JERRY I said I didn't call you about an icebox.

GITTEL [DARKLY] Whaat?

JERRY It seems I did, but I didn't.

GITTEL Look, I can't follow this whole conversation. You called—

JERRY I called because the only female voice I've heard on this phone is the robot lady with the correct time, and I'm going off my nut in solitary here. I called to make contact.

GITTEL Oh!

JERRY With someone of the weaker sex who's weaker.

GITTEL [PAUSE] Okay, here I am.

(JERRY *ponders it.*)

Contact!

JERRY I called to invite you to dinner tonight. And a show.

GITTEL So why didn't you?

JERRY I was afraid you'd say yes or no.

GITTEL Huh? I would of said sure.

JERRY See what I mean? All right, which show? It's Sunday, we'll have to see what—

GITTEL Well, now I'm *not* so sure.

JERRY Why?

GITTEL I don't know if I want to get involved now, you sound awful complicated to me!

JERRY How? Man calls to invite you to dinner via the icebox, you say there isn't any icebox, he waits to be invited in without the icebox, you show no interest in anything but the icebox, you call him back to invite him to invite you via the icebox again, he expresses interest in your personality, not your icebox, you're so devoted to the icebox you hang up. What's complicated?

GITTEL [A PAUSE] Look, what's your point?

JERRY [DRYLY] I'm kind of pointless, how are you?

GITTEL I mean I'm the girl, right? You're the man, make up your mind. *Then* ask me to dinner, and I'll make up my mind.

JERRY My point is I've been trying to make up my mind for a month here.

GITTEL What, to ask me to dinner?

JERRY To climb off a certain piece of flypaper. It's a beginning.

(*Pause*)

I mean once you break a leg in five places you hesitate to step out.

GITTEL Oh!

JERRY It's one night in the year I don't want to eat alone.

(*Another pause*)

The reason I hung up was I didn't want to say please. Help me.

GITTEL Well. How'd you expect to pick me up?

JERRY How far east are you?

GITTEL Off Second.

JERRY I'll be there in half an hour.

GITTEL Maybe you shouldn't, is it okay enough to?

JERRY Is what okay enough to?

GITTEL Your leg.

JERRY What leg? Oh.

(*He is deadpan:*)

I don't know, it seems to have affected my head. I'll see you.

(*He hangs up, replaces the phone on his couch.* GITTEL *stares, shakes her head, glances at an alarm clock on the night table, hangs up hurriedly, and darts out her door into the hall, where from another room we hear the bathtub water being turned on.*

Meanwhile JERRY'S *mood has lightened; he picks up his fallen clothes and lays them across the couch, brushes his jacket off, and slips into it. He is on his way out with his hat when the phone rings, and he comes back to answer it, thinking it is* GITTEL *and speaking dryly into the mouthpiece:*)

I'm as sane as you are, stop worrying.

(*Then his faces changes, becomes guarded.*)

Yes, this is Mr. Ry—

(*His mouth sets. After a second:*)

Who's calling from Omaha?

(*Suddenly he hangs up. He stands over the phone, his hand upon it, until it begins to ring again; then he puts his hat on slowly, and walks out of the room. He pulls the kitchen light out, and leaves, closing the outer door.*

The phone continues to ring.)

Scene 2

GITTEL'S ROOM. IT IS CLOSE TO MIDNIGHT THE SAME DAY, AND BOTH ROOMS ARE DARK, EXCEPT FOR THE LIGHTS OF THE CITY IN THE SKY BEYOND THEIR OPEN WINDOWS. THE FAINT SOUNDS OF METROPOLITAN NIGHT ARE AUDIBLE.

Under GITTEL'S *door there is a line of yellow light from the hall, where presently we hear voices and footsteps; the door is unlocked, and* GITTEL *comes in with* JERRY *behind her, both silhouetted. Their mood is light, though* JERRY'S *manner remains essentially ironic and preoccupied.*

GITTEL Look out for the furniture. Got to be a bat to find your way around *this* goddam room in the dark.

JERRY Some of my best friends are bats. And the rest are cuckoos. The—Oogh!

GITTEL There.

(*She clicks on a lamp which gives a cozy light, and tosses her purse and a theater program on the bed.* JERRY *is holding a carton of cokes and a bag, and rubbing his shin with his bandaged hand;* GITTEL *comes back, grinning.*)

So whyn't you listen?

JERRY [SURRENDERS THE THINGS] No place like home, be it ever so deadly. Sixty per cent of the accidents in this country occur in the home.

(GITTEL *takes the things into her kitchen.*)

Doesn't include ruptured marriages. Be safe, be homeless.

GITTEL [CALLING IN, AMUSED] What'll you have, coke or beer, Jerry?

JERRY Anything you're having that's wet.

GITTEL I'm having warm milk.

JERRY [WITH DOUBT] Warm milk.

(*He considers it, putting his hat on the dress dummy while* GITTEL *in the kitchen lights the gas under a potful.*)

I think I'm too old for you. I'll have a hell-bent coke.

GITTEL Coke's got caffeine in it, maybe I'll give you a beer better, huh?

JERRY Better for what?

GITTEL It's more relaxing. You had three cups of coffee at dinner, a coke now makes—

JERRY Gittel, call off the St. Bernards. I mean let's not nurse me, I've been taken care of to shreds.

(GITTEL *is brought back to the doorway by his tone, which has an edge.*)

Coke, and damn the torpedoes.

GITTEL You said you don't sleep. So you *won't* sleep.

(She goes back into the kitchen. JERRY *thinks it over, dryly.)*

JERRY It's a non-income-producing habit. If you guarantee I'll sleep with beer, you can give me beer.

*(*GITTEL *comes back into the doorway.)*

GITTEL Look, let's start all over, on your own. Coke or beer?

JERRY Warm milk.

GITTEL Now listen—

JERRY If I'm relaxing I don't want to be *casual* about it.

*(*GITTEL *shaking her head goes back into the kitchen; she continues from there, while* JERRY *explores the room.)*

GITTEL What kind of bed you got you don't sleep?

JERRY A couch I got at the Salvation Army, eight dollars.

GITTEL Well, my God, no wonder! Take a feel of that bed.

(She comes into the doorway, points with a mug; JERRY *stops to eye the bed.)*

You know how much I paid for that mattress alone? Fifty-nine bucks! Sears' best.

JERRY Six lovely feet long and wide enough for two, isn't it?

GITTEL Yeah, well, that's one thing I'd never be without is a good bed, you just got to get yourself a good bed.

(She goes back into the kitchen.)

I mean figure it out, you're in it a third of your life.

JERRY [DRYLY] You lead a very puritanical life, by that estimate.

GITTEL How come? Oh. Okay, half!

JERRY [INTERESTED] Hm. Well, I've been spending most of my nights here on the jewel-like bridges. I can't afford fifty-nine dollars just to make my bedbugs comfy.

GITTEL You got bedbugs?

(*She comes in frowning, with a box of cookies and two mugs of milk, and hands him one.*)

JERRY Among other things eating me at night.

GITTEL You out of work, Jerry?

JERRY [INSPECTING HIS MILK] I know why I'm drinking this, why are you?

GITTEL Oh, I got an ulcer.

(*She indicates her chest, explains:*)

In the duodenum.

JERRY Serious?

(GITTEL *shrugging wags her head, makes herself comfortable on the bed, her legs under her.*)

I thought ulcers in women went out with the bicycle built for two, isn't it a man's disease nowadays?

GITTEL [PHILOSOPHICALLY] Well, I got it!

JERRY Well, which are you, the old-fashioned type or the manly type?

GITTEL Why, what's the difference?

JERRY Present difference might be whether I drink this and go, or stay all night.

(He cocks an eye at her, and GITTEL *eyes him back unperturbed, a moment of frank speculation, both ways.)*

GITTEL You don't exactly lead up to things, do you?

JERRY Oh, I've been *up* for hours, pawing the ground. The only question is which way to run.

(He moves away from this subject, which leaves her perplexed; he stops to regard the gaudy bodice on the dress dummy, his manner dry and light.)

Speaking of blind as a bat, who is this for?

GITTEL Dance costume, some kid she's at the Education Alliance next Sunday.

JERRY Has no bottom part, this kid she has no bottom parts?

GITTEL Goes with tights, natch!

JERRY [AT THE SEWING MACHINE] Good idea. And here you earn an immodest living, hm?

GITTEL [DUBIOUSLY] Mmm. Half and half.

JERRY Why, what's the other half?

GITTEL The other half I'm unemployed!

JERRY [AT PHOTOS ON A WALL] Well, the answer is simple, longer costumes. Aha, acrobats. Who's the black beauty with cramps?

GITTEL That's me.

JERRY You?

GITTEL Yeah, don't act so surprised! I'm dancing.

JERRY Oh. Yes, I see. I had the impression you'd given up that line of work, or vice versa.

GITTEL [INDIGNANT] No! That's what I *am*. Ye gods, I studied with Jose for years.

JERRY Jose who?

GITTEL [STARING] Are you serious?

JERRY Good question. You mean this is the real you.

GITTEL Well, if it isn't I sure wasted a lot of seven-fifties a week!

JERRY And Mr. America here would be your ex-mistake?

GITTEL Who?

JERRY Your husband.

GITTEL Nah, Wally wasn't around long enough to *snap* a picture. That's Larry.

JERRY [SAGELY] Oh. The present mistake.

(*He contemplates the photos.*)

Somehow there's more *of* the real you. Do you have such nice legs?

GITTEL Sure! Well, I mean I did, but that's some time back, before I got sick, I lost a lot of weight since then.

JERRY [ON TIPTOE AT ONE PHOTO'S NECKLINE] With your old-fashioned duodenum? Can almost make it out in this one—

GITTEL No, ulcers you put *on* weight. That diet, ye gods, six meals a day, the last hemorrhage I had I put on eighteen pounds. I looked very good.

(JERRY *turns to her with a frown.*)

Everybody said!

JERRY The last.

GITTEL Yeah, I hope it's the last. I got just so much blood!

JERRY It is serious. How many hemorrhages have you had?

GITTEL Two. Then when I never looked healthier in my life, they had to operate on me.

JERRY For the ulcer?

GITTEL Appendicitis!

(*She becomes self-conscious under his continued gaze; she laughs.*)

No kidding, I'm a physical wreck, practically.

(*After a moment* JERRY *raises his milk to her.*)

JERRY To your physique. As is, without appendix. I couldn't resist another ounce.

(*He drinks to her, and* GITTEL *cheerfully acknowledges it with a sip of her own.*)

GITTEL So okay, that's what's wrong with me, what's wrong with you?

JERRY Me? Not a thing.

GITTEL How'd you break your leg in five places?

JERRY Oh, my leg. It broke with grief.

(*He empties the mug, sets it down, stops at her radio and clicks it on, sees that it lights up, clicks it off, and moves on, taking out a cigar.*)

GITTEL Look, whyn't you settle down and rest up?

(JERRY *turns to her, she anticipates him.*)

I'm not nursing, it just makes me nervous to watch!

JERRY [DRYLY] I have two rates of motion, the other is collapse. The last lady who invited me to settle down I couldn't get up for nine years.

(*He drops in a chair apart from her, unwrapping the cigar;* GITTEL *stares.*)

GITTEL Who was that?

JERRY Her name escapes me. The question at hand is how we're to make up our mind.

GITTEL About what?

JERRY About my staying over. I appreciate the invitation, but I'm not sure you should insist. On the other hand, it's very pleasant here and I can't plead any prior engagements.

GITTEL [A PAUSE] I don't get you, Jerry.

JERRY I only sound hard to get. No one's had much trouble.

GITTEL I mean first you can't say if you even want to eat with me, the next minute, bing, into bed. Only it's all talk, how come?

JERRY It's exploratory talk. Like the old lady who said how do I know what I think till I hear what I say.

GITTEL Ahuh. Is that the way you decide everything?

JERRY How?

GITTEL In your head?

JERRY Well, I have a little gray thingamajig in there supposed to save me false moves. Where do you decide things?

GITTEL Well, that one not in my head! I mean a couple of false moves might get you further.

JERRY [STUDIES HER FOR A MOMENT] Don't rush me. I think I should examine what I'm getting into.

GITTEL [EYEBROWS UP] Who said yes, yet?

JERRY And so should you. What if all I can afford is a—

(*He waves a hand at the photos.*)

—lady on a picture, not a whole human being with hemorrhages and so on?

GITTEL [INDIGNANTLY] So who's giving them to you?

JERRY Well. I'm burning my bridges before me. Maybe we could have a little music to obscure the future, I've missed that too.

GITTEL My God, you haven't got a radio even?

JERRY No, why?

GITTEL Everybody's got a radio!

(He lights the cigar. GITTEL *stares at him, till the radio comes in under her hand; she dials around to some music.)*

Listen, are you really broke?

JERRY [INSPECTING THE CIGAR] What kind of a name is Gittel? Has an exotic ring, Eskimo or—

GITTEL Polish. Are you?

JERRY Polish?

GITTEL Broke!

JERRY Why do you ask?

GITTEL I just want to know if that's what's keeping you up nights, and if so what'd we eat out and go to a show for? I mean we could of gone Dutch at least.

JERRY [DEADPAN] I thought you were Italian.

GITTEL Who, me? Jewish!

JERRY Mosca?

GITTEL Oh, *that's* exotic. It's my stage name.

JERRY What stage are you in?

GITTEL Huh?

JERRY What's your real name?

GITTEL Too long. For the marquees, Moscowitz.

JERRY So you became a witzless Italian. Is that where you were born?

GITTEL Italy?

JERRY Poland.

GITTEL [INDIGNANTLY] I was born in the Bronx. Listen, whyn't you get unemployed insurance? It's what I do.

JERRY Well. For one thing, I'm not a legal resident of this state.

GITTEL Oh.

(*She considers it.*)

So what state are you from, legally?

JERRY Nebraska.

GITTEL Nebraska. That's somewhere way out in California, isn't it?

JERRY I think it's Nevada that's in California.

GITTEL I mean, you're a long ways from home. You don't know anybody here you can borrow from?

(JERRY *in his chair appraises her steadily.*)

JERRY Only you.

(*A quiet moment, their eyes not leaving each other.* GITTEL *then picks up his mug, to refill it, debating.*)

GITTEL How much do you need?

JERRY [EYES DOWN] You're a very generous girl.

(*Then he gets to his feet, his voice flattening; he walks away from her.*)

Much too generous. Don't play the fairy godmother, the wolf will eat you up.

GITTEL You said you were broke!

JERRY No, you said I was broke. The unromantic fact is that last year I made fifteen thousand dollars.

GITTEL [STARING] Doing what?

JERRY I'm an attorney.

GITTEL You mean a lawyer?

JERRY Attorney. To be exotic.

GITTEL [INDIGNANT] I got eighteen bucks to get me through the month, what am I helping you out for?

JERRY [INDIFFERENT, AT THE WINDOW] Offhand I think you enjoy feeding stray wolves.

GITTEL What?

JERRY I think you're a born victim.

GITTEL Of who?

JERRY Yourself.

GITTEL [STARING] Am I wrong or have you got a nerve? I felt sorry for you, what's so terrible?

JERRY [TURNING] For me.

GITTEL Sure.

JERRY How old are you?

GITTEL Twenty-nine, so?

JERRY So. Don't talk like twenty-eight. At thirty you're over the hill, half a life gone, there's very little in this room to show for it. I think it's time you worried about your worries.

GITTEL [SCOWLING] I do! I got plans!

JERRY What plans?

GITTEL Several! I'm starting right away with this Larry, we're going to work up a whole goddam dance recital, why shouldn't we be the new Humphrey and Weidman? I'm hunting everywhere for a cheap loft to fix up a studio, I can rent it out for classes too. Not to mention I'll probably do the costumes for a show downtown, Oscar's in a new theater bunch there, he says he can—

JERRY [FLATLY] None of this will happen.

(*This is true enough to take the wind out of* GITTEL *for a moment.*)

GITTEL [INCENSED] So I'll think up something else! Why are you riding me for?

JERRY Seriously?

GITTEL Yeah!

JERRY [EVENLY] Because I enjoy you, life is short, and if you're spending it like a sailor on a spree you might as well spend some on me, but all I probably mean is trouble, I can be here today and gone tomorrow, and I'd rather not be responsible for an ingenuous little nitwit like you. In one word.

GITTEL [SCOWLING] What's ingenuous mean, smart?

JERRY Dumb. Naïve.

GITTEL Oh, for Christ sakes. I had a room of my own in the Village at sixteen, what do you think, to play potsy? All those reasons, I think you're just scared!

JERRY [A PAUSE, LEVELLY] Do you sleep with him?

GITTEL Who?

JERRY Mr. America. Larry.

GITTEL He's a *dancer.*

JERRY So you said.

GITTEL I mean we're very good friends and all that, but my God. You think I'm peculiar or something?

(*Her eyes widen.*)

Are you?

JERRY Am I what?

GITTEL Queer?

JERRY [A PAUSE, SHAKES HIS HEAD] Oh, you've gone too far.

(*He puts down the cigar.*)

No one's in your life now?

GITTEL No, I'm free as a bird, goddam it.

JERRY I'm free as a worm. We can keep it as simple as that, an item of diet.

(*His hands gesture for her, and* GITTEL *readily comes;* JERRY *kisses her. It begins temperately enough, but as* GITTEL *cooperates it becomes a wholehearted and protracted undertaking. It is* GITTEL *who slides out of it, leaving* JERRY *with his hands trembling; she is a bit jittery herself.*)

GITTEL Brother. How long you been on the wagon?

JERRY A year.

GITTEL [STARING] Where you been, in jail?

(JERRY *reaches, grasping her arms this time inexorably. He kisses her again; she resists weakly, responds, resists very weakly, and gives up, hanging loosely in his hands until they part mouths for air.*)

Look, let's not get all worked up if we're not going to finish it, huh?

JERRY Who's not going to, huh.

GITTEL I mean you just have another cookie to calm down, and then maybe you better go.

JERRY Go!

GITTEL Please.

(JERRY *releases her. A silence.*)

JERRY Is that what you meant by a false move would get me further?

GITTEL No, I—

JERRY Go where?

(*He turns away, very annoyed, finds himself at the radio, and mocks her:*)

Back to a room without a radio?

GITTEL [WEAKLY] Radio costs nineteen ninety-five—

JERRY That's cheap enough. I had the impression you'd been inviting me all night. To buy a radio?

(*He snaps the radio off, and walks.*)

GITTEL [DEFENSIVE] I got an ironclad rule I wouldn't sleep with God Almighty on the first date, you want me to be *promiscuous?* In the second place you—walk around too much—

(*She works up some indignation.*)

—and in the third place I can't stand cigars in the first place, and in the fourth place I tell you my whole life practically and what do I hear out of you, no news at all, why should I hit the hay right away with someone I don't know if he's—

(JERRY *wheels on her so bitingly it stops her like a blow.*)

JERRY *Because I'm drowning in cement here!*

GITTEL Where?

JERRY This town!

(He paces, talking through his teeth, more to himself than to her.)

I haven't passed a word with a living soul for a month, until I called Oscar—and we never liked one another! Everyone else I knew here has moved to Connecticut, Vermont, the Arctic Circle. I've worn out a pair of shoes in the museums. And a pair of pants in bad movies. And if I hike over another beautiful bridge here by my lonesome, so help me, I'll jump off! So I go back to my cell, twenty-one dollars a month, with garbage pails in the hall they'll find me gassed to death by some morning.

(He turns on her.)

And I can't *spend* nineteen ninety-five on a radio!

GITTEL [THE NEIGHBORS] Sssh! Why?

JERRY [HISSING] Because I came east with five hundred dollars. I'm living on three-fifty a day here now.

GITTEL [HISSING] You spent about sixteen-eighty on me tonight!

JERRY [HISSING] I splurged.

GITTEL What, on me?

JERRY On me. I was thirty-three years old today.

(GITTEL is speechless. He lifts up his cigar, dourly.)

So, I bought myself a dollar cigar.

GITTEL It's your *birthday?*

JERRY Sorry it—exploded.

(*He crushes it out in the ash tray.*)

GITTEL [ALARMED] So don't ruin it! You got to buy yourself a present on your birthday, my God? Whyn't you tell me?

JERRY Why, you'd like to give me one?

GITTEL Sure!

JERRY Thank you.

(*He retrieves his hat from the dummy.*)

I'm not hinting for handouts, from crackpot lovable waifs. Just don't tell a man go when you've been indicating come all night, it's not ladylike.

(*He walks toward the door.*)

GITTEL [STUNG] So what do you think you been doing right along?

JERRY [STOPS] What?

GITTEL Hinting for handouts! It's what *you* been doing all night!

JERRY Are you talking to me?

GITTEL Sure. All these hints, unhappy, bedbugs, broke—

JERRY Unhappy bedbugs!

GITTEL Unhappy! Bedbugs!

JERRY What in God's name are you dreaming—

GITTEL Like this minute, if I don't sleep with you they'll find you dead?

JERRY [ASTONISHED] Who said that?

GITTEL You did. With the garbage?

JERRY Oh, cut it out. I—

GITTEL Or off a bridge, you're so lonely? That's the *last* thing you said?

JERRY I was—I—

(But he breaks off, staring at her in less disbelief.)

That was—campaign oratory. You call that all night?

GITTEL The *first* thing you said was help me. On the phone. Right?

*(*JERRY *stares, almost speechless, though he makes one more convictionless try.)*

JERRY I—said I *wouldn't* say that, I—

GITTEL Oh, come on! You said help me, I said sure.

*(*JERRY *cannot remove his eyes from her, at a loss for words.)*

I'm not complaining, I'm used to all kinds, but what do you call me names, you want it both ways?

*(*JERRY *still stares at her, but something has opened in him that now takes him away from her, downstage, his fingers at his brow, almost in a daze.* GITTEL *becomes concerned.)*

Hey. I say something hurt your feelings?

JERRY [WITH AN EFFORT] Yes, slightly. I—

(He shakes his head, abandons the attempt at irony. Low:)

I'm remembering. Something from—

(It comes from far away, his tone now simple and vulnerable.)

—thirteen years ago yesterday. I was walking across the campus of Nebraska U, with a beautiful auburn-haired girl whose father was a sizeable wheel in the state. The girl and I were—intimate that summer, and I was telling her I'd have to leave school, no family to help me. The next day—my birthday—was the luckiest in my life, I got the George Norris scholarship. It kept me in school, and I became a lawyer. The girl and I—continued.

(*He stops.* GITTEL *waits.*)

GITTEL That's the whole story?

JERRY I married her.

GITTEL [DARKLY] You got a *wife?*

JERRY Had a wife. She's divorcing me out there.

GITTEL [CONTRITE] Oh. You too, huh?

JERRY Me too. It was just before we married I learned that Lucian—her father—had wangled that scholarship for me. You know what I said?

GITTEL What?

JERRY Nothing.

(*He opens his hands, helplessly.*)

It's absolutely true, the—point you made, you made your point.

GITTEL Which?

JERRY I ask for handouts. I never *saw* it happening before, right under my nose.

(*He shakes his head, finds his hat again, and walks once more to the door.*)

GITTEL So where you going now?

JERRY Back to solitary.

(*Beset*)

There I go again!

GITTEL So don't. Ye gods, if you hate it so much you don't want to go back there on your birthday, stay over. I got a couch in the back room, you take the bed. Maybe a good night's sleep you'll feel better in the morning, huh?

(JERRY *stares unseeing.*)

You want to stay?

JERRY Stay?

GITTEL So you'll get a good night's sleep. You'll feel better in the morning.

JERRY You mean, put you out?

GITTEL It's not out, I fit that couch. I mean you got—long legs, you know?

JERRY Yes.

(GITTEL *is eyeing his legs, with interest. When their eyes meet it is as though for the first time, really: something warmer passes between them, they are both shy about it.*)

Both of them.

GITTEL Yeah, well, I— You mind my sheets?

(*She yanks the bedspread down, takes a pillow, gathers things up.*)

I put them on clean yesterday and I had a bath.

JERRY No. It's kind of you to offer, kind of absurd, but kind—

GITTEL What do you mean absurd? You got a lousy bed,

tomorrow you'll get some kerosene and see where they come out of the wall.

JERRY Gittel. You're a very sweet girl—

GITTEL [EMBARRASSED] Well—you're a very sweet girl, too. The john's right out there behind you—

JERRY —but all I proposed was a change of bedmates.

GITTEL Listen, all *I* got in mind is a good night's sleep you'll feel better in the morning—

JERRY [SIMULTANEOUSLY WITH HER] —feel better in the morning. No doubt.

GITTEL [ALL SETTLED] So okay!

(She turns with her armful into the kitchen, puts out the light there.)

JERRY Gittel!

GITTEL [WITHIN] What?

JERRY I can't.

GITTEL [WITHIN] I'm all packed!

JERRY [A PAUSE] Crazy.

(Nevertheless, the bed attracts his eye; he turns back from it.)

Gittel!

(GITTEL reappears, still with her armful.)

Look, agree with me. It would be an act of—frailty to stay after—

GITTEL What, on your birthday?

(She goes back in. JERRY considers this argument for a long moment, contemplates the bed, and the room around it, and sighs.)

JERRY Gittel.

(GITTEL *reappears; his tone is humble.*)

Should I really stay?

GITTEL Look, don't nudya me! You want to stay?

JERRY [A PAUSE] I haven't been in a place that smelled of —human living in a month. Of course I want to stay.

GITTEL So stay!

(GITTEL *takes the hat out of his hand, drops it on the bed, gives him a towel, and disappears beyond the kitchen again. When* JERRY *opens the towel, it has a large hole in it. He shakes his head, amused, and rather forlorn.*)

JERRY I feel ridiculous.

(*He walks out into the hall, leaving the door open. After a moment* GITTEL *comes back through the kitchen, still with her armful.*)

GITTEL Listen, I—

(*She sees the room is empty, stops, stares at his hat on the bed. She scowls at it, debating. Then she shakes her head, no, no, and walks back toward the kitchen with her armful. But on the threshold she halts. After a second she turns back, and stands to give the hat another stare. Finally she sighs, and with an air of disgusted resignation mutters to herself.*)

Oh, what the hell, happy birthday.

(*And she puts everything back, her clothes back in the drawer, the clock back on the table, the pillow back in place alongside the other on the bed. She unbuttons and takes off her blouse, hangs it dangling on a chair, sits on the bed to remove her sandals, stands to slip her skirt off, walks in her half-slip and bra to a drawer again, takes out pajama-tops, and at this moment hears* JERRY *in the hall; she skedaddles with the pajama-tops into the darkness beyond the kitchen.*

JERRY *returns, and walks around, restive. It is a moment before he accidentally kicks one of* GITTEL'S *sandals, stares at them, then at her skirt on the floor, then at her pillow next to his, and looking toward the kitchen, comprehends her intention. He takes up her blouse in his fingers. Bringing it to his face, he inhales the odor of woman again; he rubs it against his cheek, thinking, scowling. At last he comes out of the other end of some maze, and tells himself grittily:*)

JERRY It's, not, a, *beginning.*

(*He hangs the blouse back on the chair, turns, picks up his hat from the bed, and walks straight out into the hall, closing the door behind him.*

After a moment GITTEL *peers in from the kitchen, clad in the pajama-tops and carrying her underthings; she sees the room is still empty and comes in. Quickly she clicks off the lamp, turns down the sheet, has her knee up to get in, remembers, and kneels around to the foot of the bed with her hand outstretched for* JERRY'S *hat. It is not there. She searches, baffled, then sees the door is now closed; she scrambles over the bed to it, looks along the hall to the john and then down over the bannister. Two stories down, there is the closing of the street door.*

GITTEL *comes back into her doorway, where she stands silhouetted; after a perplexed moment she slaps her thigh, in resignation.)*

Scene 3 BOTH ROOMS. IT IS SEVERAL HOURS LATER, AND THE FIRST LIGHT OF DAWN IS JUST BEGINNING TO PICK OUT THE FURNITURE IN BOTH ROOMS.

GITTEL *is in her bed, asleep, with the blanket and sheet pulled up over her ears.*

JERRY'S *room is empty, but after a moment we hear* JERRY *letting himself in at his door. When he opens it, he spies and bends to pick up a telegram waiting inside the threshold. He comes into his living-room staring at it, unkempt, needing a shave, weary from walking all night, but relatively lighthearted. He takes the telegram to the broken window, tears the envelope open, then pauses in the act of lifting the message out, and presently shoves it back in, tosses it onto his couch, and lights a cigarette. He walks around a few steps, then stands deliberating between the telegram and the phone, and suddenly sits to the phone. He dials, waits.*

The phone in GITTEL'S *room rings.* GITTEL *rolls around before she is altogether awake, her hand fumbling till it finds the phone.*

GITTEL [EYES CLOSED] Yeah, h'lo.

(JERRY *considers how to begin.*)

H'lo!

JERRY [DRYLY] About that icebox. I think you let that other jerk have it too cheap.

GITTEL Whah?

JERRY If you keep handing things out to the first comer, judgment day will find you without an icebox to your name, morally speaking.

GITTEL [JERKING UP] Jerry! Hey, you all right? I called you two three times, no answer.

JERRY I tried another bridge. Queensboro, it opens a vast new territory to—

(*He catches himself, breaks off.*)

I was about to say get lost in, but that's my last hint. I walked out on you, Gittel.

GITTEL Yeah. I noticed!

JERRY What changed your ironclad rule?

GITTEL Oh—I couldn't resist your goddam hat!

JERRY I should have left it for you. I thought it was something else.

GITTEL Like what?

JERRY Charity. I think your trouble is running the community chest.

GITTEL Huh?

JERRY My trouble is my wife does understand me. You lit a fair-sized birthday candle under me tonight, it cast a light backwards all the way to Omaha, Nevada.

GITTEL How?

JERRY Tess—her name is Tess, it comes back to me from time to time—also smothered me in loving kindnesses. But my God, if I hinted for them it's not all her fault. I needn't have gone into her father's law office. I needn't have let him set us up in a handsome house in Fairacres. It poisoned the well.

GITTEL [SCOWLING] Well?

JERRY Well—we had running water, but not much monogamy. I had to be heroic with some wife, no matter whose, and Tess now is marrying someone else, a colleague of mine who—

(*He breaks this off.*)

That's another chapter. I wanted to say only that tonight half my life looks like a handout, and I finally walked out on one. From you.

GITTEL Oh. *I* thought it was something else.

JERRY Such as?

GITTEL I figured you figured I wasn't—

(*She takes a breath.*)

I mean maybe you didn't think I was— You know.

JERRY No.

GITTEL Attractive!

JERRY [A PAUSE] Oh, God. And you still called me two or three times?

GITTEL [SHE HAS HER PRIDE] *Two* times.

JERRY Why?

GITTEL Well, you disappear like that, I got worried about you.

JERRY Gittel.

(His tone is gentle, very affectionate, for the first time genuinely heedful of her; the relationship is taking on a quite different color.)

Gittel, I'll tell you two truths. One, you're attractive, two, you don't look out for yourself.

GITTEL Sure I do.

JERRY No. If you did you'd object more.

GITTEL What to?

JERRY So many things. This minute, this very minute, why aren't you taking my head off about the time?

GITTEL Why, what time is it?

JERRY Little before five. It takes practice, go ahead.

GITTEL Go ahead what?

JERRY Practice. Protest. Enter an objection.

GITTEL Huh?

JERRY *Holler* at me!

GITTEL What for?

JERRY It's a hell of an hour to phone anyone. Who do I think I am, waking you up this time of night, my father-in-law? It shows no respect for you, you resent it, say so!

GITTEL Look, what are you hollering at me for?

JERRY [MILDLY] Your own good.

GITTEL I don't like to holler at people, it makes me nervous. Anyway, I'm glad you phoned.

JERRY Why?

GITTEL [EXASPERATED] What makes you so dumb? *I was worried about you!*

JERRY That's better.

GITTEL Better!

JERRY All you need is practice. Go ahead.

GITTEL [IRATELY] Who's practicing? What do you think, I'm nuts, you know what time it is, is that what you call me up five o'clock in the morning to practice hollering?

JERRY [AMUSED] No, I called to say don't give anything else away. Until I see you.

GITTEL What?

JERRY I'm asking whether you'd—care to try being half of a pair?

GITTEL [A PAUSE] Look, let's not go through all *that* again!

JERRY On my terms, this time. And I don't mean as a hand-out.

GITTEL So what do you mean?

JERRY That *I'd*—like to look out for you. Hemorrhages notwithstanding.

(GITTEL *stares at the phone.*)

Will you let me?

(GITTEL *shakes her head, too uncertain about her feelings to know what to say; she is touched, and also wants to snicker.*)

GITTEL I'm—I— Why?

JERRY I think you can use me. Not that I'll be such a bargain, a lot of me is still tied up in the—civil wars. I thought I'd tell you the whole mess, if you'd have breakfast with me.

GITTEL Where?

JERRY Here. Will you come?

GITTEL Well, I'm having a tooth pulled out eight-fifteen. I mean I'll be spitting a lot of goddam blood, we won't be able to *do* anything.

JERRY Will you come?

GITTEL Sure I'll come.

JERRY [A PAUSE, GENTLY] I'll look for you.

(*He is about to hang up, when he has an afterthought.*)

Gittel.

GITTEL Yeah?

JERRY What do you do when a tooth bleeds?

GITTEL [CONCERNED] Why, you got one?

JERRY Oh, you're a character. I'm talking about *yours.*

GITTEL Oh. Let it bleed, why? It dries up.

JERRY I knew I'd have a use for that icebox. I'll have a cake of ice in the sink.

GITTEL What for?

JERRY For the ice bag I'll buy for your tooth.

GITTEL [A PAUSE, AMUSED] You're starting right in, huh?

JERRY Not a minute to lose. It's a new day, in my thirty-fourth year, and I feel like a rising lark. Get some sleep, now.

(*He hangs up.* GITTEL *sits for a moment, then also hangs up and shakes her head in a kind of wonderment.*)

GITTEL Sonofabitch.

(*Presently she gets up and goes into her kitchen, pours herself some milk from the pot, and comes back; she settles in bed with it.*

JERRY *sets his phone on the floor and remains smiling, until his eyes again encounter the telegram. He picks it up, fingers it. Finally he draws it out, takes it to the window, and reads it. He goes over it twice in silence; the third time he reads it aloud to himself, without expression.*)

JERRY "I called to say happy birthday you stinker don't shut me out God help both of us but will you remember I love you I do Tess."

(*After a second he perceives the telegram is trembling. He crumples it in his hand, and drops it slowly out the broken window. He returns to his couch, transfers his clothes to the chair, and lies down to finish his cigarette.*

Each lies alone with his thoughts in the bleak light of daybreak, JERRY *smoking and* GITTEL *sipping her milk; the only sound is some distant church clock ringing five.*)

ACT TWO

Scene 1

JERRY'S ROOM. IT IS OCTOBER NOW, EARLY EVENING, DUSK.

GITTEL's room is much the same, with her bed unmade and two pillows rumpled; but a transformation has overtaken JERRY's. It has been fixed up inexpensively, and now is tidy, pleasant, livable, with bedspread, wall lamp, throw rugs, burlap drapes, stained fruit crates for shelving—all improvements in the peasant style of GITTEL's garb. Near the window there is a bridge table with two chairs, set for dinner. GITTEL's little radio is playing on a shelf, WNYC, symphonic music.

The light in the kitchen is on, now agreeably shaded; out here GITTEL, wearing a dishtowel for an apron, is preparing dinner. She comes in carrying a bowlful of salad, sets it on the table, and stands listening thoughtfully to the music; she then has a kind of slow convulsion, which after a moment we see is a modern-dance movement, because she stops, is dissatisfied, scratches her head, tries another, gives it up, and returns to the kitchen. Here she opens the gas-range oven to peer in, does some basting, closes it. In the middle of her next turn she halts, listens towards the door, then skedaddles back in and hastily begins lighting two candles on the table. We then see JERRY *opening the outer door.*

GITTEL [CALLING HAPPILY] Hiya, baby.

JERRY Hi.

(*He stops to sniff the oven, looks in.*)

Hmm. Smells good, who's in here? Chicken!

GITTEL And salad, and potatoes, and wine's on the ice.

JERRY Wine, well.

(*Coming into the doorway he leans there, just taking her in at the candles; he is in street clothes and hat, with a legal tome or two under his arm, and some parcels.*)

What are we launching, me?

GITTEL I got a bargain, sixty-nine cents a bottle. Must of been getting kind of old.

(*She comes to kiss his amused face above her, and his arm draws her in.*)

What's so funny?

JERRY You are, infant.

(*He spies the window over her shoulder.*)

You put up curtains for me!

GITTEL Sure, what do you think I come over for, just to see you?

JERRY Very cozy. Last couple of weeks you've turned this into the show place of the nation. You're better than wine, you improve with age.

GITTEL What's in the bag?

JERRY Everything's in the bag.

GITTEL I mean this bag.

JERRY Don't move!

GITTEL [ALARMED] Huh?

JERRY Careful. Back in one inch.

GITTEL Why?

JERRY [SOBERLY] Because all afternoon I've been totally surrounded by lawbooks, and I like it much better being totally surrounded by you. I got your thread.

(*He jiggles a bag at her ear.*)

GITTEL Oh, good. You see Frank Taubman, Jerry?

JERRY I did. And dessert.

(*He jiggles another bag.*)

Soya cake. Salt-free, butter-free, flavor-free.

GITTEL Well, what'd he say?

JERRY You'll hear. And a piece of the moon. From me, to you.

(*He deposits the third bag in her hand.*)

GITTEL A present?

JERRY Just a piece of the moon.

(GITTEL *unwraps it at the candles, while* JERRY *gets rid of his books and hat, takes off his jacket.*)

GITTEL I can't wait to see what's in it, what's in it?

JERRY [DEADPAN] Well, it turns out this way, she opens this box from her lover thinking it's candy but it's really the preserved brains of her unfaithful father, who has run away to join this gang of juvenile delinquents, she recognizes him instantly and lets out an unearthly shriek—

GITTEL [BLANKLY, LIFTS IT] A cake of soap?

JERRY [APPROACHING] Supposed to be the preserved brains of—

GITTEL What's the matter, I smell?

JERRY Good idea, let's investigate.

(*He puts his nose in her hair from behind, his arms around her waist.*)

GITTEL I mean what kind of present is a cake of soap, I need a bath?

JERRY What kind of present is a— Did you look at the box?

GITTEL No.

JERRY Read the soap.

GITTEL [BY CANDLELIGHT] Channel number—

JERRY Channel number five, it's a TV sample. Chanel number five, girl, you're holding a two-fifty soap bubble there.

GITTEL [AGHAST] Two-fif— For *one* cake of soap?

JERRY Don't you dare take a bath with that. We're going to eat it, spoonful by spoonful. Instead of that soya cake.

GITTEL You know sometimes I think the nutty one of this twosome some of us think I am is you? Two-fifty, we won't eat!

JERRY We'll eat, it will be a feast. How's your belly?

GITTEL Oh, fine. I took some banthine, it went away.

JERRY Didn't all go away. Here's some.

GITTEL Some what?

JERRY Belly.

GITTEL Oh. You think I'm too fat.

JERRY Good God, no.

GITTEL You think I'm too skinny?

JERRY [DRYLY] I think you're a sacred vessel of womanhood.

GITTEL Ahuh. Sexy as all get-out, that's why you buy me a hunk of soap.

JERRY Buoyant in the bow, swivelly in the stern, and spicy in the hatch, how's that?

GITTEL S'pretty good.

(*They have been kissing; now* GITTEL *cocks her head back.*)

You think I'm *too* sexy?

JERRY Hm?

GITTEL I mean oversexed?

JERRY I think you're a mixed-up girl. Calmly considered, your bottom is tops.

GITTEL Some vessel. Sounds like a shipwreck.

(*She kisses him again. When they come up for air, she slides out of his hands.*)

Anyway! You're getting a phone call soon. Long-distance.

JERRY Who from?

GITTEL [BRIGHTLY] Your wife.

(*She inhales at the soap again.*)

This her kind, Jerry?

JERRY [A PAUSE] No. And I seldom gave her gifts, she was—amply supplied.

GITTEL Okay.

(She takes the soap out into the kitchen, busies herself at the oven. JERRY *stands alone, not moving, for a long moment; then he calls out, sounding casual.)*

JERRY When did she call?

GITTEL [CALLING IN] Soon's I got here. Said she'd call back eight o'clock.

*(*JERRY *looks at his wrist watch, stares at the phone, clears the litter off the table, glances again at the phone, and goes to his window, to gaze out.* GITTEL *comes back in, bearing a casserole of chicken and a bowlful of French fries to the table, with cheerful chatter.)*

She must have money to burn, huh? I mean *two* long-distant phone calls, ye gods. You know I only made one long-distant phone call in my whole life?

(She stands serving out their portions.)

Tallahassee, that's in Florida, right after we were married. Wally had a job there. I mean he said he had a job, when I found out it was really a redhead he went back to I didn't drop dead either, but I called him up—

JERRY I don't think I care to talk to her.

*(*GITTEL *continues serving, but frowning over it.)*

Gittel.

GITTEL So don't. Anyway I got the bill, that's when I did drop dead.

JERRY I won't answer.

GITTEL [PRESENTLY] All right. You want to get the wine?

JERRY With pleasure.

(He turns the radio on, and goes into the kitchen.)

Let's drink life to the dregs, the whole sixty-nine cents worth. I have something for us to toast. I had a long session this afternoon with Frank—

(GITTEL meanwhile stares at the phone, then switches the radio off; the mood in the room changes, and the phone now begins to haunt what they do and say. JERRY returns with the wine and a corkscrew.)

What's the matter, honey?

GITTEL [SITS] I don't see any crowd.

JERRY That I said I wouldn't answer?

GITTEL Nothing's the matter!

JERRY It's dead and buried.

(He uncorks the bottle.)

Six feet under, the coffin is sealed, the headstone is paid for, I'd rather not open it all up again.

(Lightly)

Let's change the subject to something pleasant. How are you making out on your recital?

GITTEL That's pleasant? I looked at that loft again—the goddam bastard still wants a two-year lease and won't come down a cent. I mean I haven't got that kind of gelt. It's a very fine dance studio, for Rockefeller.

JERRY You don't need Rockefeller, you have Fort Knox here.

GITTEL Where?

JERRY [TAPS HIS BROW] I had a long session with Frank Taubman this afternoon.

GITTEL So what'd he tell you?

(But her look is on the phone.)

JERRY That if I'm not a member of the New York Bar he could offer me only some briefs to prepare.

GITTEL Oh.

JERRY I'll go down with you in the morning and we'll give this goddam bastard two months rent.

GITTEL Out of what?

JERRY I accepted them. It pays per brief, we'll be papering the walls with gelt.

GITTEL I'll get the loft when *I* get a job.

(Her look again is on the phone; this time JERRY *notices.)*

JERRY [A PAUSE] It didn't say anything.

GITTEL Huh?

JERRY The phone.

GITTEL Yeah. I heard Schrafft's was putting on girls, I'm going to see about it tomorrow.

JERRY Schrafft's. Waiting on table?

GITTEL Whatever they got. I worked the candy counter for them last year, I put on seven pounds. It's very good candy.

JERRY Do me a small favor, let me do you a small favor?

GITTEL Sure. Like what?

JERRY Like stake you to Loft's, instead of Schrafft's. You know how much I can earn doing briefs? A hundred a week, I'll *buy* you candy. It's absurd for you to work at Schrafft's.

GITTEL What have you got against Schrafft's?

JERRY I'm afraid someone there will eat *you* up. No Schrafft's, the prosecution rests.

(*They eat again.*)

You know this chicken is fabulous? What makes it taste like gin?

GITTEL Gin.

JERRY Fabulous. You can sew, you can cook, you—

(*He suddenly takes note, ominously.*)

What are we doing eating French fries?

GITTEL You like them.

JERRY Not after you were up half the night with a belly-ache.

GITTEL [INDIGNANT] You said they were your favorite.

JERRY [MILDLY] My favorite will put holes in *your* stomach lining. And your stomach lining is my favorite, how many did you eat?

GITTEL Three.

JERRY [RISES] Three too many.

GITTEL I love them.

JERRY [HESITATES] Four is all you get.

(*He lifts the potatoes from her plate in his fingers, drops one back and takes the bowlful out into the kitchen.*)

GITTEL Hey!

(But the protest is weak, she contents herself with snaring others from JERRY's *plate in his absence, and pops them into her mouth. He comes back with a slice or two of bread.)*

JERRY Here. Instead. You need starch to soak up the acids, honey, I've been reading up on the whole pathology of ulcers and you simply don't know what to do with your acids. In medical parlance we call this a half-acid diagnosis. Let's stick to what *you* can eat, hm?

GITTEL [HER MOUTH FULL] Certainly!

*(*JERRY *about to sit consults his wrist watch, frowns, glances at the phone; then, sitting, finds* GITTEL's *eyes on him.)*

It didn't say anything!

JERRY What?

GITTEL The phone.

JERRY Not going to, either. I was just thinking I'd forgotten the sound of her voice. How did she sound?

GITTEL [SCOWLING] What do you mean how did she sound?

JERRY [BORED] Only how did she sound, don't—

GITTEL Lovely, she sounded lovely! You want to hear how she sounds, talk to her. What are you scared of?

*(*JERRY *puts down his fork, and contemplates her.)*

JERRY [EVENLY] You really want me to answer it, don't you?

GITTEL Who, me?

JERRY Why?

GITTEL Why not?

JERRY Because I'm in a state of grace here in a garden of Eden with you and a stuffed chicken. Adam and Eve, and you know what that twelve hundred miles of phone cable is? the snake. Why let it in, it was enough work getting rid of the bedbugs.

GITTEL Why do you hate her so?

JERRY I don't, let's change the subject.

(*They eat again.*)

I'll go with you about this loft tomorrow. Tell the man I'm your lawyer, I handle nothing but your leases, I'll negotiate the whole transaction. I'll even bring my brief case.

GITTEL What kind of bread is this?

JERRY Health bread. For our health.

GITTEL Gee, they must cut this right off a *stump*, huh?

(JERRY *sits back and enjoys her.*)

JERRY You're a bug. A water bug, this way, that, what did I do to have you in my blood stream? Look. I'm saying if you're a dancer it's time to do something about it, the days are going—

GITTEL [VEHEMENTLY] Of course I'm a dancer, it's driving me crazy! Everybody else is getting famous, all I'm getting is repair bills from Singer's!

JERRY All right then, I can lend a hand with the loft. You go to work on the recital, I go to work on the briefs.

GITTEL What's doing briefs?

JERRY Researching a case for precedents.

(GITTEL *is uncomprehending, so he clarifies it.*)

When one cuke brings suit against another cuke, the court can't decide which cuke is cukier until it hears how two other cukes made out in *another* court in 1888.

GITTEL So is that fun?

JERRY Not unless you have a nose-in-the-book talent. But I needn't be writing briefs for the rest of my life, I can practice in court here any time I take the state Bar exam.

GITTEL So whyn't you take it?

JERRY [SMILES] It makes me nervous.

GITTEL Aah. You'd knock them dead.

JERRY What makes you think so?

GITTEL [SERENELY] I got my impressions.

JERRY I barely know the traffic laws here. Statutory law *varies*, from state to state, I—

GITTEL So what, you could study up.

JERRY [DRYLY] I'm a little old to go back to school.

GITTEL Every day you read in the paper, some grandma going to NYU, eleven grandchildren, seventy years—

JERRY Do I look like somebody's grandma? I'm not *that* old, but I've been a practicing—

(*But he breaks off and leans back to regard her for a moment. Then:*)

How do you do it?

GITTEL What?

JERRY We begin with my saying I'll lend a hand, and end one minute later with you putting me through college.

GITTEL I don't need a hand, I'll make out!

(JERRY *is displeased with this, and after a moment lowers his face to his plate.*)

You got to take the exam sometime, no?

JERRY No.

GITTEL So what'll you be here in your old age?

JERRY Don't rush me into the grave. I'm not living that far ahead.

*(*GITTEL *is displeased with this, and after a moment lowers her face to her plate. They eat.* GITTEL *then bounces up, marches into the kitchen, returns with the bowl of potatoes, and drops a fistful into her plate.)*

GITTEL What are you, on vacation here?

(She sits. JERRY *reaches over, puts the fistful back into the bowl, rises, and carries it out again to the kitchen. He returns without it.)*

JERRY Not necessarily, but I *might* die somewhere else. Be a shame to go to all the trouble of taking the Bar exam in New York and die in New Jersey. I'd have to commute.

(He sits. GITTEL *rises, and marches toward the kitchen again; but* JERRY *catches her wrist, pulls her onto his lap.)*

Look, look.

(He reaches a long arm out to the couch, catches up one of the legal tomes, and deposits it open on GITTEL's *thighs. She scowls at the text.)*

GITTEL What?

JERRY This is Clevenger. Civil Practice Act of New York, what I don't know fills this little volume and a library full besides. To take the Bar exam here. For two days in this state they lift open the top of your skull and stare in. Now—

GITTEL Jerry, you know what I think you got too much of? Lack of confidence!

JERRY Oh, great.

GITTEL I mean ye gods, you were such a popular lawyer in Nevada, what's the difference?

JERRY Nebraska, dear.

(*He kisses her neck.*)

GITTEL Nebraska, so what's the difference?

JERRY About a thousand miles. You know you have a two-fifty smell without that damned soap?

GITTEL [SQUIRMS] Giving me goose-pimples. Jerry, now I'm talking seri—

(JERRY *turns her face, kisses her; after a moment she comes up for breath.*)

—ous, how come you were so popular there if—

JERRY [KISSING HER THROAT] I shot in the mid-seventies.

GITTEL [STARES] Shot what?

JERRY [KISSING HER CHIN] Birdies.

GITTEL That made you *popular?*

JERRY In the butterfly set.

(*He kisses her mouth; this time she comes up with her eyes closed, takes a breath, and gives up.*)

GITTEL Oh, damn you.

(*She seizes his ears and kisses him fiercely; Clevenger slides to the floor, unnoticed, and the kiss goes on. Now the phone rings.* GITTEL'S *head comes up. After a second* JERRY *draws it down with his hand, but the next ring brings her up scowling at it.)*

Phone's ringing.

JERRY [LIGHTLY] I don't want the world in.

(He draws her to him again; it rings again.)

GITTEL I can't!

*(*JERRY *puts her aside on her feet, gets up, crosses, takes the phone off the hook, drops it to hang and comes back.)*

JERRY Better?

GITTEL Oh, for Christ sakes.

(She ducks past him, and picks up the phone, combative.)

Yeah, hello. . . .

JERRY [OUTRAGED] Put down that phone!

GITTEL . . . So whyn't you call sooner— . . .

*(*JERRY *coming swiftly snatches the phone from her, ready to slam it down.)*

It's *Larry!*

*(*JERRY *stares at her, lifts the phone to his ear, listens, then hands it to her, and walks away.)*

Hello? . . . No, we thought it was the—landlord. So what'd the Y say? . . . *How much?* . . .

*(*JERRY *stands staring out the window, which is now dark with night;* GITTEL'S *eyes are on him.)*

Well, listen, I can't— . . . No, maybe we'll try Henry Street, but I can't think about it now. . . . I'm in the middle of eating, Larry, I'll call you back later. . . . No, I can't swing the loft yet, but I can't go into all that now.

(*She hangs up and stands over the phone.* JERRY *leaves the window; at the table he drains his tumbler of wine in one swallow, sets it down. They stand silent for a moment,* GITTEL *not taking her eyes from him.*)

JERRY [CURTLY] I'm sorry I shouted.

GITTEL What did that bitch do to you?

JERRY [ROUNDING] Bitch?

(*Grimly, then*)

Married me, helped put me through law school, stood by me in pinches. Loved me, if anyone did or could. She was never a bitch, don't call her that again.

GITTEL [NETTLED] That's why you left Nebraska, she was so nice?

JERRY I left because I couldn't take being in the same town with her and her fiancé.

GITTEL So you ran away.

JERRY If that's what you call starting over from bedrock, yes, I ran away.

GITTEL So stop running, it's the Atlantic Ocean already.

JERRY No one's running now.

GITTEL You're running, why can't you talk to her on the phone?

(JERRY *turns to look at her.*)

JERRY Ask it of me. Don't do it for me, ask it of me, perhaps I'll do it for you. Do you want me to?

GITTEL She's your wife.

JERRY Do you want me to?

GITTEL It's your phone.

JERRY Do *you* want me to? Yes or no!

GITTEL No!

JERRY [A PAUSE] You want me to work here for Frank Taubman?

GITTEL No.

JERRY What *do* you want from me?

GITTEL Not a goddam thing.

(*She lights a cigarette, takes a drag.* JERRY *passing removes it from her lips, and* GITTEL, *very annoyed, shakes another from his pack while he is stubbing the first out.*)

JERRY Why do you smoke, you know it's not good for your stomach.

GITTEL I'll keep track of my own stomach, we been together almost thirty years now, we get by!

(*She strikes the match to the new cigarette and* JERRY *turns. He observes her, not moving a muscle, until it comes in an outburst.*)

JERRY Don't be such a damfool tower of strength!

GITTEL What!

JERRY I'm sick of it too, idiotic act of taking care of you and your weak stomach. Weak, you're as tough as wire.

GITTEL So one of us better be!

(JERRY *stares at her grimly; when he speaks now it is level, but unsparing.*)

JERRY And one of us better not be. You don't get by, you only tell yourself lies. From day to day, sure, job to job, man to man, you get by. And nothing sticks, they take off to Tallahassee. Did you pay his train fare?

(*This is a mock question, but* GITTEL'S *open mouth is a real answer.*)

My God, you did! You pay the freight, and every bum climbs on for a free ride. And you never know why the ride is over, do you? I'll tell you why, when a man offers you a hand up you put a donation into it. Why don't you spit in it? So they use you and walk out. How many of them have you slept with on their way through, twenty-five?

(*He waits.*)

Fifty?

(GITTEL *only stares, now he is inexorable.*)

Five hundred? It's not a lark any more, you're not a kid, you're on the edge of a nightmare, and you're all alone. Who cares, but me? Don't spit in my hand, Gittel, whether you know it or not you need it. And make one claim, one real claim on a man, he just might surprise you.

(*He waits:* GITTEL *continues to stare, palely, not answering.* JERRY'S *voice is hard:*)

Do you get my point?

GITTEL [SHAKEN] Sure.

(*Then she reacts, leap-frogging over her own feelings:*)

You're a *terrific* lawyer, what are you bashful about?

JERRY You didn't understand one word I—

GITTEL Sure I did, and if I was the jury I'd send me up for five years, no kidding.

(*She rises, escaping toward the kitchen;* JERRY *catches her wrists.*)

JERRY *I'm* not kidding!

GITTEL So what do you want? Let go my—

JERRY Need someone!

GITTEL Let me go, Jerry, you're hurting—

JERRY Need someone!

GITTEL For what? Let go my arms or I'll yell!

JERRY You won't yell. Now you—

GITTEL *Help!*

(JERRY *drops her wrists. She stumbles away from him, tears of pain in her eyes, and inspects her wrists.*)

JERRY You little lunatic, someone will come.

GITTEL Nobody'll come, it's New York.

(*But her voice is trembling as she shows her arm.*)

Look, I'm going to be all black and blue, you big ape! I ought to get out of here before you slug me.

JERRY Slug you. Is that something you've learned to expect from your romances?

GITTEL I expect the worst! When it comes to men I expect the worst!

(*Now she is struggling against the tears.*)

Whyn't you pick up the phone if you're so goddam strong?

JERRY Do you want me to?

GITTEL I don't know where I stand here, it's a big question mark, why should *I* stick my neck out?

JERRY [INEXORABLY] Do you want me to?

GITTEL I *will* get a job too, what's such a crime, just—cause I—won't—

(And finally the tears come; helpless with sobs she turns away, trying to keep her weeping as private as she can, and failing.)

JERRY [MOVED] Gittel, I—shouldn't have said all that—

GITTEL [WHEELING ON HIM] All right, all right, I can scream my head off here and nobody comes, who can I count on besides me?

JERRY Me, Gittel.

(The phone rings. JERRY *alone turns his eyes to it; he stands unmoving.* GITTEL *gets her sobbing in hand, and waits on his decision. It rings again, and at last she speaks.)*

GITTEL You. Lean on you I'll fall in a big hole in Nevada somewhere.

(She comes to the table to crush the cigarette, but JERRY *stops her hand; he takes the cigarette from her, goes with it to the phone, and lifts the receiver.)*

JERRY Yes? . . . Yes, speaking. . . .

(A pause, while the connection is made; GITTEL *stands, and* JERRY *takes a much-needed drag.*

His head comes up with the voice at the other end.)

Hello, Tess. . . .

(*His own voice starts out deliberately casual.*)

No, I didn't care to talk to you the other times, I'm doing it now by special request. . . . What's that, woman's intuition? . . . Yes, she is. . . .

(GITTEL *now moves to clear the dishes from the table, very quietly; she takes a stack out to the kitchen.*)

Her name's Gittel . . . I do, very much. . . . I didn't plan to be celibate the rest of my days, wouldn't do you any good. . . . And a year of it in your house didn't do me any good. . . .

(*Sardonically:*)

Oh, I'll be glad to represent you in the divorce. If your father will represent me, I need a good lawyer to help take him to the cleaners. . . .

(*Now more irritable:*)

Oh, tell him to stuff it up his—safe-deposit box, if I need money I can earn it . . . I have a job, I accepted one today. A girl, an apartment, a job adds up to a life, I'm beginning. . . . I have no intention of contesting the divorce, tell Lucian he can file any time, I'll enter a voluntary appearance. The sooner the better . . . I'm not interested in being *friends* with you and your fiancé, you'll have to put up with each other. . . .

(*Now through his teeth:*)

Tess, you can't sink a knife in me and hope to leave a tender afterglow. . . .

(*Watching him with the cigarette we see what this conversation is coming to cost him; he controls himself. Now weary:*)

Tess, are you calling me halfway across the continent to talk about the furniture? . . . If the house is haunted burn it, we'll split the insurance. . . .

(GITTEL *comes back in to clear what remains on the table. Now shakily:*)

I'm not unfeeling, *I* don't want to be haunted either, my God, you made a choice, *get your hand out of my bowels!* . . .

(GITTEL *stiffens at this.* JERRY *closes his eyes in pain.*)

Tess. . . . Don't. . . . Please—plea— . . .

(TESS *hangs up.* JERRY *looks at the phone, and slowly replaces it; he is drenched in sweat, and sudden tears confuse his eyes; when he lifts his hand for a prolonged drag, the cigarette is shaking. He does not look at* GITTEL. *She reaches with her fingers and pinches out each of the candles; the room goes dark except for the light from the kitchen.* GITTEL *without a word lies face down on the couch, and does not stir.*)

Gittel.

(GITTEL *is silent.* JERRY *comes to stand above her, puts a hand on her hair; she huddles away.*)

Gittel, I—

GITTEL [SUDDENLY] It's not what you think!

JERRY What isn't?

GITTEL Larry says the Y wants six hundred and twenty-five bucks for one night, that's where we been saying we'd give it. I can't even get up sixty-five a month for a lousy loft!

(*Another silence*)

JERRY [SHAKILY] No. Let's look at the snake.

(*He tugs the string to the overhead bulb, and its naked light floods the room. He stands, unsteady.*)

Gittel. Turn around. Please.

(*She lies unmoving.*)

Look at me!

(*She rolls half around now, to face him with her eyes smouldering.*)

Don't pretend. It hurts, let me see it hurts—

GITTEL What, what?

JERRY How I can—drown in that well. I need you.

GITTEL For what?

JERRY Give me something to hold onto! How do I climb out, where do I get a—foothold here, who do I work *for*, what do I build on? I'm in limbo here and I'm—shaking inside. Gittel. Need *me* for something, if it's only a lousy loft.

(GITTEL *keeps her eyes on him for a long moment; then she comes through in kind, almost inaudibly.*)

GITTEL Sure it hurts. I'll never hear you tell me that.

JERRY What?

GITTEL That I got a—hand inside you.

JERRY [A PAUSE] Meet me halfway.

(*Presently* GITTEL *smiles, wryly.*)

GITTEL You mean in that loft, huh? Okay. Now put out that goddam light, will you?

(JERRY *tugs it out.*)

C'mere, you—French fry potato.

(*He comes, she clasps him around the neck, and pulls him down upon her; and they lie in the haven, rack, forcing-bed of each other's arms.*)

Scene 2

BOTH ROOMS. IT IS SEVERAL WEEKS LATER, NOON, A COLD DECEMBER DAY. IN BOTH ROOMS THE HEAT IS NOW ON—IN GITTEL'S FROM A GAS HEATER AFFIXED TO THE WALL, IN JERRY'S FROM A NEW KEROSENE STOVE IN THE CENTER OF THE FLOOR.

GITTEL'S *room is empty, the door ajar.* JERRY *is in his room, lying in a spread of legs and legal papers on the couch, with the telephone receiver tucked at his shoulder, in the middle of a conversation.*

JERRY . . . Yes. . . . Well, that was the issue in McCuller *v.* Iowa Transfer, if a claimant not the consignee enters— . . . That's right, they appealed and it was reversed. This outfit doesn't stand a Chinaman's chance of collecting out there, Mr. Taubman, I don't— . . . Hm? . . . All right: Frank. I don't think we should even consider a settlement . . . It's not going out on a limb. Though many a lawyer would have a fresh view of things from the end of a limb, I— . . . Why, thank you. . . . No, the surprise is finding myself such an expert here on Midwest jurisprudence. . . . I see what it proves, it proves an expert is a damn fool a long way from home. . . .

(*The phone in* GITTEL's *room rings.*)

No, taking the Bar exam is something I need about as badly as a brain operation, what for? . . . Why should they admit me to the Bar on motion? . . . I'm familiar with the procedure, you sponsor me and I deliver a truckload of Nebraska affidavits. Maybe I can get the affidavits, I'm doubtful about the truck. . . . If it saves me taking the Bar exam why not, but why should you sponsor— . . . Full time. I see. . . . How much would you pay me?—just to keep it symbolic. . . . 6500 what, two-dollar bills? . . . Not enough, Mr.—Frank. If I'm useful to have around full time I'm worth at least 7500, and to nail me down will take eight, so we'd have to begin talking at nine. . . .

(GITTEL's *phone rings again.*)

I might be very serious, I'm interested in being nailed down. . . . But not to the cross, by a Bar exam. If you'll sponsor me on motion, I'll certainly see what affidavits I can dig out of Omaha— . . .

(GITTEL *meanwhile runs in from the hall, to answer her phone; she is clad in a nondescript wrap, and we see her countenance is adorned with a white mustache-smear and goatee-dab of bleaching cream. Her mood is listless.*)

GITTEL Yeah, hello? . . . Oh, Sophie, hiya. . . .

JERRY [GLANCING AT WRIST WATCH] . . . Yes, I can take a cab up. . . .

GITTEL . . . Good thing you called, how long am I supposed to leave this stuff on? I look like a goddam Kentucky colonel here. . . .

JERRY . . . No, I was going to bring this Wharton brief in after lunch anyway. . . .

GITTEL . . . It itches. . . .

JERRY . . . All right, men's grill at the St. Regis, quarter past. . . .

GITTEL . . . What old friend? . . . Sam? . . .

JERRY . . . Yes. See you.

(He clicks down, again consults his watch, and dials.)

GITTEL . . . What'd you tell him I'm going steady for? I mean how do *you* know I'm going steady if I don't know? . . . So let *me* shoo them off. . . . I don't know what I sound worried about, I sound worried? . . .

JERRY [BUSY SIGNAL] Come on, Sophie, get off that damned line.

(He hangs up, and without collecting his things walks out of his flat.)

GITTEL . . . Well, my stomach's been giving me a pain in the behind. . . . No, everything's peachy. . . . Oh, she's going to marry someone else. . . . I don't *know* how I get involved in such a mix-up, anyway it's not such a mix-up. . . . No, Wally was different. . . . Milton was different. . . . Which Max? . . .

(She locates her mug of milk, and takes a swallow.)

Look, did anybody ever buy me a loft before? . . . Yeah, *he* used to bring me a Mr. Goodbar, that one still owes me seventy-two bucks I'll never see again. The fact is I'm a born victim! Here I am, practically thirty years old, I'm just finding it out. . . .

(JERRY *returns with a fistful of mail, among which is a feminine blue envelope; it stops him. He discards the others, rips it open and reads it, troubledly.*)

So who's *against* going steady? . . . What do you think, I'm crazy? Take him home to meet Momma he'll leave New York in a balloon. . . . You don't understand—he plays *golf*, for instance. I never knew anybody personally played golf. . . . Oh, what do *you* know? . . . He's got a lot on the ball! He busts his brains all day over these briefs he's doing, then he comes down the loft and sweeps up for me, what do you think of that? . . . Sure! I made twenty-two bucks on that loft this month, and Molly's got this kids' class she's going to move in this week. . . .

(JERRY *consults his watch again; he returns to the phone and dials, one digit.*)

JERRY Operator, I want to call Omaha, Nebraska, Atlantic 5756. . . .

GITTEL [DISPIRITED] . . . Yeah, I been working on my recital. Well, trying to. . . .

JERRY . . . Algonquin 4-6099. . . .

GITTEL . . . It's hard to get started again after so long, you know? . . .

JERRY . . . Call me back, please.

(He hangs up, then slowly lifts the letter to his nostrils, in a faraway nostalgia.)

GITTEL . . . Maybe I'll take up golf instead. . . . Sure he talks to her. . . . About the divorce, she won't get off the pot! . . . Sophie, I *told* him talk to her, he *has* to talk with her, what are you bending my ear about? . . . Sophie, you're getting me mad. . . . Cause you're pestering me! . . . So don't be such a friend, be an enemy and don't pester me!

(She hangs up irately, and commences to dial again. Before she completes the round, Jerry's phone rings; he answers it.)

JERRY Yes? . . . All right. . . .

GITTEL [BUSY SIGNAL] Oh, nuts.

(She hangs up, gathers some clothes, and goes into her back room.)

JERRY . . . Hi, Ruth, is your boss in? . . . Tell him it's his son-in-law. The retiring one. . . . Thank you, Ruth, I miss you folks too. . . . Hello, Lucian, how are you, don't answer that question. . . .

(He moves the phone out from his ear.)

No, I have a job, thanks, in fact I'm applying for admission to the New York Bar on motion. . . . Sure, tell Tess. She thinks the only feet I can stand on are hers. . . . I'm calling about her. I have a letter from her here, it has a St. Joe postmark. What's she doing in St. Joe? . . .

(He moves the phone out from his ear.)

Well, it didn't walk down there and mail itself. I've had a call in to her since Wednesday, there's nobody in the house. When did you see her, Lucian? . . . Drives where for three days? . . . Just drives? . . . I wish you'd spend more time around her, you're better than nothing. . . . I mean your idea of solicitude is a loud voice, Lucian, just talking to you on the phone is like a workout with dumbbells. . . .

(*He moves the phone out from his ear.*)

Money isn't enough. I have too much to say on that, though, sometime I'll call you collect. . . . She's not all right, I can smell it between the lines here. . . . What girl? . . . Of course I have a girl here, I told Tess so. . . . You mean it's since *then* she's so— . . . Devastated by what? . . . My God, Lucian, I waited for a year, a solid year, till I didn't have an ounce of self-respect left in me! One ounce, I packed with it. . . . Is that her word, abandoned? Tell me how I can abandon another man's bride, I'll come to the wedding. . . . Lucian, listen. Keep an eye on her, will you? That's all I called to say. . . . And give her my best.

(GITTEL *comes out of her back room, dressed for the street.* JERRY *hangs up, collects his topcoat, hat, and brief case, consults his watch, then hurries to dial.* GITTEL *picks up her phone, commences to dial, and* JERRY *gets a busy signal.*)

Oh, hell.

(*He hangs up, as* GITTEL *completes dialing, and hastens out of his flat. His phone now rings once, twice, while* GITTEL *in her room stares at her phone with mounting indignation. On the third ring* JERRY *comes running back in, and grabs up his phone just in time to hear* GITTEL *addressing hers:*)

GITTEL Ye gods, you were just there!

JERRY I'm here.

GITTEL Oh, Jerry!

JERRY I called twice. Hasn't Sophie got anything better to do than to talk to you?

GITTEL No. I called *three* times, who you been yakking with?

JERRY I was talking to Omaha.

GITTEL What, *again?*

(A *pause*)

JERRY What does that mean? I had a peculiar letter from Tess, she—

GITTEL You ask her about the divorce?

JERRY No. It was Lucian, I didn't get to the divorce. Tess seems sunk, her father says she—

GITTEL [HASTILY] Jerry, I'm on my way to the loft, I got to hurry, what are you calling me about?

JERRY I thought you were calling me.

GITTEL Who?

JERRY Never mind. I called Lucian because I had to know what's going on out there, he says Tess has shut herself off from—

GITTEL [INTERRUPTING] Jerry, I got to run, you give me a ring tomorrow.

JERRY [STARING] What about tonight?

GITTEL It's Friday, after the loft I'm going to Momma's.

JERRY What's special about Friday?

GITTEL Gefüllte fish, good-by.

JERRY [PROTESTING] Hey, we had a dinner—

(*But* GITTEL *hangs up.* JERRY *looks at the empty phone, his voice dying.*)

—date.

(After a moment he also hangs up. GITTEL *backs away from her phone, while* JERRY *glances at his watch; each is reluctant to leave.* GITTEL *halts,* JERRY *hesitates over his phone, both are tempted to try again; but neither does. After a melancholy moment they turn and leave, in opposite directions.)*

Scene 3

GITTEL'S ROOM. IT IS FEBRUARY NOW, A SATURDAY NIGHT, LATE. BOTH ROOMS ARE DARK, AND THE GLOW OF THE CITY PLAYS IN THE SNOWY NIGHT OUTSIDE THE WINDOWS.

For a moment there is no movement in either room.

Then there is the sound of a key at GITTEL'S *and the door swings open.* GITTEL *is silhouetted in the doorway, alone and motionless, resting against the jamb from brow to pelvis; then she pushes away, and comes unsteadily in. There is a sprinkling of snow on her hair and overcoat. She lets her purse drop on the floor, weaves her way around the bed without light except from the hall, and in the kitchen gets herself a glass of water at the sink; she drinks it, fills another, brings it in, and sits on the bed, with head bowed in her hand. After a moment she reaches to click on the lamp, takes up her address book, and searches for a number. She dials it, and waits; when she speaks her voice is tired and tipsy.*

GITTEL Dr. Segen there? . . . *I'm* calling, who are you? I mean are you really there or are you one of these answering nuisances? . . . So can you reach Dr. Segen for me? . . . Yeah, it's an emergency. . . . Gittel Mosca, I used to be a patient of his, will you tell him I'm very sick? . . . Canal 6-2098. . . . Thanks.

(*She gets rid of the phone, and still in her overcoat, drops back onto the bed. The lamp-light is in her eyes, and she puts up a fumbling hand to click it off. She lies in the dark, an arm over her face. After a second* JERRY *in topcoat and hat comes silently up, around the bannister in the hall, and into the doorway, where he stands. The snow has accumulated thickly on him. He sees* GITTEL'S *purse on the floor, picks it up, sees the key still in the lock, and draws it out; it is this sound that brings* GITTEL *up on her elbow, startled, apprehensive.*)

Oh! Hiya, Jerry. Where'd you blow in from?

(JERRY *regards her, his manner is heavy and grim, and hers turns light.*)

How was *your* party, have a good time?

JERRY Not as good as you. Are you drunk, at least?

GITTEL [WITH A GIGGLE] I had a couple, yeah. I had this terrible thirst all night, you know, I didn't stop to think. I mean think to stop.

(JERRY *drops the key in her purse, tosses it on the bed, and closes the door; he walks to the window, silent, where he leans against the casing, not removing his hat.)*

JERRY [THEN] Let's get it over with, who was the wrestler?

GITTEL What wrestler?

JERRY The fat-necked one who brought you home just now.

GITTEL Jake?

(She sits up.)

He's not a wrestler, he's a very modern painter.

JERRY That's why you kiss him goodnight, you're a patroness of the arts?

GITTEL [STARING] Where were you?

JERRY One jump behind you. In more ways than one.

GITTEL I didn't kiss him, he kissed me. Didn't you go to Frank Taubman's party—

(She pushes herself to her feet, changes her mind, and sits again, shivering.)

Light the gas, will you, honey, I'm awful cold.

*(*JERRY *after a moment takes out matches, and kneels to the gas heater. When it comes on, it illuminates* GITTEL *drinking the glass of water in one gulp;* JERRY *rising sees her, and comes over to grip her wrist.)*

JERRY You've drunk enough.

GITTEL It's water!

*(*JERRY *pries her fingers loose, and tastes it. He gives it back.* GITTEL *grins.)*

What's the matter, you don't trust me?

JERRY Trust you. You were in his cellar in Bleecker Street for an hour.

GITTEL [STARING] How do you know?

JERRY What was he showing you, great paintings, great wrestling holds, what?

(GITTEL *does not answer, and* JERRY *yanks on the lamp, sits opposite her on the bed, and turns her face into the light.*)

What?

(*She only reads his eyes and* JERRY *reads hers, a long moment in which she might almost cry on his shoulder, but she ends it with a rueful little snigger.*)

GITTEL So what do you see, your fortune?

JERRY Yours. And not one I want to see. You look trampled, is that what you're in training to be?

GITTEL [IRKED] Ye gods, I had about six drinks, you think I'm ruined for life?

JERRY I don't mean anything so wholesome as drink. You slept with him, didn't you?

GITTEL Whyn't you take off your hat and stay awhile?

(*She pushes his hat back from his eyes, then touches his temple and cheek.*)

Poor Jerry, you—

JERRY [PUTS HER HAND DOWN] You slept with him.

GITTEL You want to cry? I want to cry.

JERRY [GRIMLY] Differences aren't soluble in tears, this city would be one flat mud pie. *Did* you sleep with him?

(*But* GITTEL *rolls away into a pillow, her back to him.*)

GITTEL We both know I'm dumb, whyn't you talk plain words a normal dumb person could understand?

JERRY How plain, one syllable?

GITTEL Yeah.

JERRY Fine. Did he lay you?

(GITTEL *lies averted in silence, her eyes open.*)

I asked did he—

GITTEL So what if he did, that's the end of the world?

(*Now she does rise, to get away from him, though she is wobbly, and soon drops into a chair.* JERRY *puts his fingers to his eyes, and remains on the bed; it takes him time to come to terms with this.*)

JERRY Maybe. Of this world.

(*But he can't hold the anger in, he smacks the glass off the night table and is on his feet, bewildered and savage, to confront her.*)

Why? *Why?*

GITTEL [WEARILY] What's it matter?

JERRY It matters because I'm at a crossroads and which way I send my life packing turns on you! And so are you, you want to watch *your* life float down the sewer out to sea? You care so little?

GITTEL I don't know, I—

JERRY For me?

GITTEL Oh, Jerry, I—

JERRY For yourself?

GITTEL Myself, I got other things to worry—

JERRY Why did you *want* to?

GITTEL I don't *know* why! Anyway who said I did?

JERRY [*Glaring at her*] You'll drive *me* to drink. *Did you or didn't you?*

GITTEL Well, he may of slept with me, but I didn't sleep with him.

(JERRY *stares at her, tight-lipped for patience.*)

JERRY All right, let's go back. Why did you go home with him?

GITTEL It's a long story, I used to go with Jake two three years ago—

JERRY Not that far back. Get to tonight.

GITTEL So tonight I had a couple of drinks too many, I guess it was—just a case of old lang syne.

JERRY Old lang syne—

GITTEL *You* know.

JERRY Yes, I'm an expert in it, especially tonight. Why did you drink?

GITTEL [BORED] You're supposed to be at the Taubman's having a good time.

JERRY Is that why?

GITTEL Nah, who wants to go there, for God's sake.

JERRY I went about this trouble with the affidavits. I left as soon as I could to pick you up at Sophie's, you were just coming out with him, giggling like a pony.

GITTEL [INDIGNANTLY] I was plastered, I said so, you want a *written* confession?

JERRY You don't get plastered and flush us down the drain for no reason, and Taubman's party isn't it. I'm after the—

(*She gets up wearily, again to move away from him.*)

Don't walk away from me! I'm talking to you.

GITTEL So go ahead, talk. Lawyers, boy.

JERRY Because when something happens to me *twice* I like to know why. I'm after the reason, what did I do this time, what's your complaint?

GITTEL Who's complaining? *You* are!

JERRY My God, I have no right?

GITTEL Don't get off the subject.

JERRY It's the subject, I'm talking about you and me.

GITTEL Well, I'm talking about your wife!

(*A silence.* GITTEL *walks, rubbing her stomach with the heel of her hand.* JERRY *quiets down, then:*)

JERRY All right, let's talk about her. She's interested in you too, I feel like an intercom. What about her?

GITTEL I saw your last month's phone bill. Omaha Neb 9.81, Omaha Neb 12.63—Whyn't you tell me you were the world's champion talkers?

JERRY I like to keep in touch, Gittel, she's having a very rough time.

GITTEL So who isn't? I got a headache, lemme alone.

JERRY What's your case, I'm unfaithful to you with my wife over the phone, it's the phone bill pushes you into bed with this what's his name jerk?

GITTEL Jake.

JERRY Jerk! It could be you're pushing me into Grand Central for a ticket back, has that thought struck you? Is that what you want, to cut me loose? So you can try anything in pants in New York you've overlook—

(But GITTEL *has flopped across the bed, face down, and lies still and miserable.* JERRY *contemplates her, his anger going, compassion coming, until he resigns himself with a sigh.)*

All right. All right, it can wait till tomorrow. We'll battle it out when you're on your feet.

(He drops his hat on a chair, comes over to the bed, kneels and begins untying her shoes. This kindness sends GITTEL *off into a misery, her shoulders quiver, and she whimpers.)*

GITTEL Oh, Jerry—

JERRY What's the matter?

GITTEL You don't like me any more.

JERRY I hate you, isn't that passionate enough? Turn over.

*(*GITTEL *turns over, and he starts to unbutton her overcoat; her hands come up, his ignore them.)*

GITTEL I can do it.

JERRY It's a huge favor, have the grace not to, hm?

GITTEL [DESISTING] You don't hate me.

JERRY I wouldn't say so.

GITTEL You just feel sorry for me.

JERRY What makes you think you're so pathetic? Pull.

GITTEL [FREEING ONE ARM] Ever saw me dancing around that loft, boy, you'd think I was pathetic. I been sitting on that goddam floor so many hours I'm getting a callus, I wait for ideas to show up like I'm—*marooned* or something. So the dawn came, after all these years, you know what's wrong?

JERRY [PAUSING, GENTLY] You're not a dancer?

GITTEL [STARING] How'd you know?

JERRY I didn't. I meant that loft as a help, not just to puncture a bubble.

GITTEL So if I'm not a dancer, what am I?

JERRY Is that why you got crocked? Turn over.

(GITTEL *turns back over, and he slips the coat from her other arm and off; he begins to unbutton her blouse in back.*)

Will you drink coffee if I make some?

GITTEL [SHUDDERING] No.

JERRY Or an emetic? Get the stuff off your stomach?

GITTEL You mean vomit?

JERRY Yes.

(GITTEL *now, breaking away from his fingers in sudden vexation, rolls up to glare at his face.*)

GITTEL Why we always talking about my stomach? I got no other charms?

(JERRY *reaches again.*)

Get away!

(*She pulls the still-buttoned blouse over her head, gets stuck, and struggles blindly.*)

JERRY [COMPASSIONATELY] Gittel.

(His hands come again, but when she feels them she kicks out fiercely at him.)

GITTEL [MUFFLED] I don't want your goddam favors!

(One of her kicks lands in his thigh, and stops him. GITTEL *then yanks the blouse off with a rip, slings it anywhere, which happens to be at him, drags the coat over her head on her way down, and lies still. A silence)*

JERRY [THEN] I'm sorry you don't. I could use it.

(He retrieves the blouse, draws the sleeves right-side out, and hangs it over a chair, then stands regarding her.)

That's how you intend to sleep it off?

*(*GITTEL *under the coat neither moves nor answers.)*

Gittel?

(Again no answer)

You want me to stay or go?

(After a wait JERRY *walks to his hat, picks it up.)*

Go.

(He looks at the gas heater, pauses.)

Shall I leave the gas on?

(No response from under GITTEL*'s coat.)*

Yes. You need me for anything?

(He waits.)

No. Of course not.

(Presently he puts the lamp out, walks around the bed to the door, and opens it. But he stands. Then he bangs it shut again, throws his hat back at the chair and walks in again after it. GITTEL *then sits up to see the closed door, and gives a wail of abandonment.)*

GITTEL Jerry—Jerry—

JERRY [BEHIND HER] What?

*(*GITTEL *rolls around, to see him staring out the window.)*

GITTEL [INDIGNANT] What are you still here?

JERRY I *can't* put it off till tomorrow.

(He catches up a newspaper and rolls it in his hands as he paces, grimly. GITTEL *kneels up on the bed and regards him.)*

GITTEL What's ailing *you?*

JERRY I have to talk. I called home today.

GITTEL So what'd she say for herself this time?

JERRY I didn't talk to her.

(He paces.)

I can't get the court affidavits I need there unless I ask her father to pull strings for me. I called to ask, and couldn't get my tongue in the old groove.

GITTEL So hooray.

JERRY Yes, hooray. It means the Appellate Division here won't admit me, on motion. I want my day in court. I've got to get out from behind that pile of books into a courtroom, and I'm at a dead end here. With one way out, the March Bar exam.

GITTEL So take it.

JERRY I'm *scared.* I've been under Lucian's wing all my professional life, I'm not sure myself what's in my skull besides his coattails, if I take that exam I'm putting everything I am in the scales. If I flunk it, what?

GITTEL What else can you do?

JERRY [SLOWLY] I can live where I *am* a member of the Bar.

(GITTEL *stares at him, and neither moves; then she sits back on her heels.*)

GITTEL [UNBELIEVING] You want to go back.

(*The phone rings.* GITTEL *glances at it with sharp nervousness, knowing who it is, then back at* JERRY.)

Go on.

JERRY Answer it.

GITTEL No. Go on.

(*It rings again, and* JERRY *walks to it, the roll of newspaper in his hand.*)

Let it ring! I won't talk to anybody.

(*Her alarmed vehemence stops* JERRY, *he stares at her. The phone rings a few times throughout the following, then ceases.*)

JERRY [SHARPLY] Who is it, this late, him?

GITTEL I don't know. So you going or not?

JERRY [ANGERED] Why not? I can make three times the

money I earn here, to do the work I'm starved for, it tempts me and what's so tempting here, Jake? Beat my head against a Bar exam when I'm building here on what, Jake, kicks in the belly, quicksand?

(GITTEL *offers no answer. He turns back to the window.* GITTEL *now digs in her purse for a bottle of banthine tablets.*)

GITTEL What do you think *I'm* up to my neck in here, not quicksand?

(*She goes out into the kitchen, where she puts on the light and sets a pot of milk up to warm;* JERRY *turns after her.*)

JERRY All right, then tell me that! If something sticks in your throat you can't spit it out? It's so much quicker to hop in with the first gorilla you meet instead? How *dare* you treat yourself like a hand-me-down snotrag any bum can blow his nose in?

(GITTEL *is shaken by this; but she avoids him and comes back in, cool as metal, unscrewing her bottle of tablets.*)

GITTEL Okay. When?

JERRY When what?

GITTEL When you going?

JERRY [HEAVILY] Look. Don't rush *me* off to Tallahassee. I don't turn loose so easy.

GITTEL Well, I got to make my plans.

JERRY What plans, now?

GITTEL [UNCONCERNEDLY] I'll probably hook up with Jake again. He's got a lot to give a girl, if you know what I mean, you'd be surprised.

(JERRY *stands like a statue,* GITTEL *with a not unmalicious twinkle gazing back at him. Then his arm leaps up with the roll of newspaper to crack her across the side of the head, it knocks her off balance and the bottle of tablets flies out of her hand in a shower; she falls on the bed.*)

JERRY [FURIOUS] That's not all I mean to you! *Now tell the truth, once!*

(GITTEL *holds her cheek, never taking her eyes from him.* JERRY *then looks around, stoops and picks up the tablets and bottle, reads the label, sees what it is. He goes into the kitchen. He pours her milk into the mug, and brings it back in. He hands her the mug, which* GITTEL *takes, still staring at his face while he weighs the tablets in his palm.*)

How many?

GITTEL Two.

(JERRY *gives her two, and she swallows them with a mouthful of milk. He replaces the others in the bottle.*)

JERRY If your stomach's bothering you, why don't you go to a doctor?

GITTEL What do I want to go to the doctor? He tells me don't have emotions.

(JERRY *screws the cap back on the bottle, tosses it on the bed, and regards her.*)

JERRY How bad is it?

GITTEL It's not bad!

JERRY Did I hurt you?

GITTEL Sure you hurt me. What do you think my head's made, out of tin?

(She waits.)

You didn't say you're sorry.

JERRY You had it coming. Didn't you?

GITTEL Sure.

JERRY I'm sorry.

(GITTEL now takes a sip of milk, holding it in both hands like a child; then she looks up at him with a grin.)

GITTEL You see? I said you'd slug me and you did.

JERRY Makes you so happy I'll oblige every hour.

GITTEL [RUEFULLY] Who's happy? Boy, what a smack.

(She explores her cheek, tentatively, with one palm.)

Okay, so you're *not* going!

(She eyes him cheerfully, but JERRY turns away from her.)

JERRY I didn't finish.

(He stands at the window, to gaze down at the street.)

Now the divorce plea is in, Tess is in a—tailspin. Lucian thinks she won't remarry.

(This is worse than being hit, and GITTEL can only sit and stare.)

GITTEL [AT LAST] Oh, brother. You stand a chance?

JERRY Maybe.

(But he shakes his head, suddenly wretched at the window:)

I don't know what or where I stand, what to put behind me, what's ahead, am I coming or going, so help me, I—

(He breaks it off. GITTEL *hugs her shoulders together, she is cold; it takes her a moment to find desperation enough to try to go over the edge.)*

GITTEL All right, Jerry, I'll tell you the truth. I—

(She looks for where to begin.)

About tonight and Jake, I—did want to go to Frank Taubman's. Only I don't fit in with your classy friends. Like she would.

*(*JERRY *turns and looks at her.)*

JERRY What?

GITTEL What do you think, I don't know?

(She is hugging herself, shivering a little as she makes herself more naked, but trying to smile.)

I mean all I am is what I am. Like Wally, he wanted me to get braces on my teeth, I said so face it, I got a couple of buck teeth, what did I keep it, such a secret? I said you got to take me the way I am, I got these teeth.

JERRY You're a beautiful girl. Don't you know that?

GITTEL But I'm not her. And she's all you been thinking about since the minute we met.

JERRY No.

GITTEL Yes. So what's Jake, a—piece of penny candy. It's like when I was a kid, we used to neck in the vestibule, she's inside you and I'm always in the vestibule! You never gave me a chance. Okay, but then you say need you. I need you, I *need* you, who has to say everything in black and white?

(*She rises to confront him, pressing the heel of her hand into her stomach.*)

But if you want I should of just laid down and said jump on me, no, Jerry. No. Cause I knew all the time you had it in the back of your head to—prove something to her—

JERRY To myself.

GITTEL To her. Everything you gave me was to show her, you couldn't wait for a goddam *letter* to get to her. So when *you*—ask *me* to—hand myself over on a platter—

(*She has endeavored to be dispassionate, but now it is welling up to a huge accusatory outcry:*)

For what? For *what?* What'll I *get?* Jake, I pay a penny, get a penny candy, but you, you're a—big ten-buck box and all I'll get is the cellophane! *You shortchange people, Jerry!*

(JERRY *takes this indictment moveless, but rocked, staring at her.* GITTEL *hugs herself, tense, waiting till she has hold of herself.*)

And that's the truth. That's what you did *this* time.

(*A silence. She waits upon him, intent, still tense, so much hangs on this; while he absorbs it painfully in his entire anatomy.*)

JERRY [THEN] You mean I want a—complete surrender. And don't give one.

GITTEL Yeah. Is that all I said?

(JERRY *closes his eyes on her.*)

JERRY This time. And last time too. Because I shortchanged her also, didn't I?

GITTEL [DESPERATE] I'm not talking about *her* now, that's exactly what I'm talking about!

(*But it takes* JERRY *unhearing away from her to the bureau, averted.* GITTEL *gives up, sits, slaps her chair, and puts her head in her hands.*)

JERRY It's true. God help me, it's true, half of me isn't in this town.

GITTEL So I tried Jake.

JERRY Of course.

GITTEL Okay, a snotrag. So we're both flops.

JERRY Both?

(*And presently he nods. But when he turns his gaze to her, and takes in her forlorn figure, his eyes moisten.*)

No. Not altogether.

(*He comes to stand behind her; she does not lift her head.*)

All these months I've been telling you one thing, infant, you live wrong. I wanted to make you over. Now I'll tell you the other thing, how you live right.

(*He gazes down at her hair, moves his hand to touch it, refrains.*)

You're a gift. Not a flop, a gift. Out of the blue. God knows there aren't many like you, so when he makes one it's for many poor buggers. Me among many.

(*He shakes his head, slowly.*)

The men don't matter. I promise you, *the men don't matter.* If they use you and walk out, they walk out with something of you, in them, that helps. Forget them, not one of them has dirtied you. Not one has possessed you, nobody's even got close. I said a beautiful girl, I didn't mean skin deep, there you're a delight. Anyone can see. And underneath is a street brawler. That some can see. But under the street brawler is something as fresh and crazy and timid as a colt, and virginal. No one's been there, not even me. And why you lock them out is—not my business.

(*He finds his hat, stands with it, not looking at her now.*)

What you've given me is—something I can make out with, from here on. And more. More. But what I've given you has been—What? A gift of *me,* but half of it's a fraud, and it puts you in bed with bums. That colt needs an unstinting hand, infant. Not Jake, not me.

(*He walks to the door, opens it, pauses, looking for a final word, and gives it across his shoulder.*)

I love your buck teeth.

(*After a moment he starts out, and* GITTEL'S *head comes up.* JERRY *is on the stairs when she stumbles around her chair, and cries out the doorway after him.*)

GITTEL Jerry! Don't go!

(JERRY *halts, not turning.*)

The main thing *I* did in Jake's was—faint in the john. That's when I found I—

(*Her voice breaks, the tremor in it is out as a sob.*)

I'm bleeding, Jerry!

JERRY [WHEELS ON THE STAIRS] What!

GITTEL It's why I was so thirsty, I'm—scared, Jerry, this time I'm scared to be bleeding—

JERRY Gittel!

(*He runs back in, to grip her up by the arms; she leans on him.*)

GITTEL Help me, Jerry!

JERRY [STRICKEN] Who's your doctor?

GITTEL It's all right, you just got to get me to the hospital—

JERRY *Who's your doctor?*

GITTEL Segen. In my book, it was him calling, I didn't want you to know—

JERRY You *lunatic.* Lie down, you—crazy, crazy—nitwit—

(*He turns her to the bed, where she lies down;* JERRY *sits with her, and looks for the number in her book.*)

GITTEL [WEEPING] Jerry, don't hate my guts.

JERRY Why didn't you *tell* me?

GITTEL I didn't want to trap you—trap you in anything you—

JERRY Trap me? *Trap* me?

GITTEL I hate my goddam guts, I'm so ashamed, but don't leave—

JERRY Oh God, shut up, you—lunatic girl—

GITTEL Don't leave me, don't leave me—

JERRY I'm not leaving!

(He finds the number, bends to her face on his knee.)

I'm *here*, infant. Take it easy, can't you see I'm here?

(He kisses her; then he commences to dial with his free hand, GITTEL *pressing the other to her cheek.)*

ACT THREE

Scene 1

GITTEL'S ROOM. IT IS MARCH NOW, MIDDAY, SUNNY AND WARM.

JERRY's room has an unused look—the window is closed and the shade pulled down, a pillow in its bare ticking lies on the couch, the curtain drawn back on the clothes-closet corner reveals chiefly empty hangers.

In GITTEL's room the window is open and the sunlight streams in. The furniture has been rearranged. JERRY's suitcase is in a corner. The sewing machine and dress dummy are gone, and in their place is a table littered with lawbooks, mimeographed sheets and syllabuses, notebooks, pencils in a jar, a desk lamp, JERRY's portable typewriter, a coffee cup, a dirty plate or two, a saucer full of butts. The night table by GITTEL's bed has become a medicine table, studded with bottles and glasses, including one of milk; a new and more expensive radio is also on it, playing softly.

GITTEL *herself in a cotton nightgown is in bed, pale, thin, and glum. She lies with her head turned to gaze out the window. The hefty book she has been trying to read rests on her lap, her finger in it, and she is not hearing the radio, until the music stops and the announcer begins, cheerfully. What he has to say is that this is WQXR, the radio station of* The New York Times, *to be fully informed read* The New York Times, *and wouldn't she like to have* The New York Times *delivered every morning before breakfast so she could enjoy its world-wide coverage while sipping her coffee, join the really smart people who—*

GITTEL [DISGUSTED] Aah, shut up, what do you know.

(She dials him out, and gets some music elsewhere; but she is in no mood to listen, and clicks it off altogether. She then opens the book again, and scowls with an effort of concentration over the page. But she heaves first a gloomy sigh, and next the book: it hits the floor and almost hits a flinching JERRY, *who is opening the door with his foot, his arms laden with lawbooks and groceries, his topcoat over his shoulder, his hat back on his head.* GITTEL *brightens at once.)*

JERRY Hold your fire, I'm unarmed!

GITTEL Jerry, honey, I thought you'd never be home.

*(*JERRY *bends to kiss her, then drops his lawbooks and coat and a gift box on the table. Throughout the scene he attends to a variety*

of chores in an unpausing flow, without leisure really to stop once; he is in something of a fever of good spirits. He indicates the gift box.)

JERRY I came home a roundabout way, to bring you something from China. Though they met me more than halfway.

GITTEL You don't have to bring presents.

JERRY After lunch. I got in a tangle with old Kruger on this Lever contract, I have to be back by one.

(He bears the groceries out to the kitchen.)

GITTEL [DARKLY] That's two minutes ago.

JERRY Yes, if I hurry I'll be late. I had a great morning though, I bore down on the old barracuda and he only opened his mouth like a goldfish. All those barracudas seem to be shrinking, lately, must be the humidity. What kind of morning did you have?

GITTEL So so.

JERRY [NOT APPROVING] Just lay here?

GITTEL I almost got up to go to the john.

JERRY Ah, that will be the day, won't it?

GITTEL Yeah. Be in all the newsreels.

(JERRY in silence in the kitchen lights the oven, unwraps a small steak, slides it under the broiler.)

I'll try for the john tomorrow, Jerry, I'm pretty wobbly.

JERRY What do you expect the first time, to climb Mount Everest?

GITTEL [A PAUSE] *That's* what they go up there for?

(*She gazes out the open window, while* JERRY *opens a can of potatoes, and dumps them in a pot to warm.*)

You know where I'd like to be this minute?

JERRY In bed, or you'd be out of it.

GITTEL Central Park. On the grass. I don't get any *use* out of Central Park, you know? Specially a day like this, I mean here spring isn't even here and spring is here.

(JERRY *comes back in, unknotting his tie, en route to the bureau to rummage in its drawers.*)

JERRY I'll make you a proposition, will you shoot for the stairs by Friday afternoon?

GITTEL [UNEASILY] Why?

JERRY I called Dr. Segen again this morning, he emphatically recommended a change of venue. I'll take you to Central Park in a cab Friday afternoon, is it a date?

GITTEL What's Friday afternoon?

JERRY The exam's over, I'd like to collapse in Central Park myself. Be down to get you in a taxi, honey, straight from the Bar exam. Date?

GITTEL [EVADING IT] One thing I'll be glad when that exam's over, maybe you'll stop running long enough to say hello.

JERRY [OBLIGES, WITH A SMILE] Hello. Date?

GITTEL [SCOWLING] I just sit on the edge here, I feel like my stomach's a—cracked egg or something. I don't want any more leaks.

(JERRY *gives her a severe eye while he hangs his jacket over a chair and takes a batch of mail out of its pocket.*)

JERRY Doctor says if you don't get out of bed this week all your blood will rust. I really couldn't afford that hello, I didn't have a minute yet to look into who's writing me what here.

(He hurries through the envelopes, discarding them one by one onto the bed.)

Harper's wants me to buy their complete works, haven't time to read why. Hospital bill, ouch. Smoke it after dinner, on the gas stove. Clerk of the District Court, Omaha—

(But this one stops him short. He carries it away from her, rips it open, unfolds a legal document, in blue backing distinctive enough to be remembered later, and stares at it.)

GITTEL Anything?

JERRY [A SILENCE] Legal stuff. Coming out of my ears these days, I—

(He finds it difficult to lift his eyes from it, it takes him an effort, but he drops document and envelope on the table and gets back into stride.)

Here, before I forget.

(From his jacket he brings a check out and over to GITTEL.*)*

I let Molly's class in the loft, she gave me a check for you. She'll leave the key over the door, I'll pick it up before cram-school.

GITTEL Gee, Jerry, you shouldn't take time.

(She takes his hand as well as the check, and puts her cheek to it.)

You're okay.

JERRY It's your money I'm after, infant.

GITTEL [BRIGHTLY] Yeah, it pays to be a big fat capitalist, huh? Lay here, it just rolls in.

JERRY [STOOPING] And this rolls out. Get up today or forever hold your peas.

(He comes up with a bedpan from under the bed, and bears it into the back room, while GITTEL *stares.)*

GITTEL Hey, what's the—My God, I lost a quart of blood!

JERRY I bought you three pints, that's a handsome enough profit. Capitalists who aren't satisfied with fifty per cent end up in the federal hoosegow.

(On his way back he picks up the book and a mimeographed exam sheet that has fallen out of it.)

What are you doing with this exam, boning up for me?

GITTEL Just looking.

JERRY [SCANNING] '53, I'll have to go through this one tonight.

(He drops the novel and exam sheet back on the bed, strips to the waist, now at last removes his hat and sets it on the desk lamp, and collects the dirty plates and saucer of butts, while GITTEL *watches him.)*

GITTEL When you going to get some sleep? You're getting skinny!

JERRY Muscle, I'm all muscle these days. And that reminds me, if you don't get off your rear end soon I'll be advertising in the Sunbathers Gazette for one that works.

(He bears the plates into the kitchen, where he next opens the oven and turns the steak over.)

GITTEL [SCOWLING] Mine works.

JERRY Unemployed. You think unemployed insurance can go on in perpetuity?

(This is only kidding, while he proceeds to splash water into his face at the sink; but GITTEL *staring into the future is so despondent she has to shake it off.)*

GITTEL So when have you got any time, *now?*

JERRY Three-thirty Friday after the battle, mother. Date?

GITTEL In Central Park?

JERRY [NOT HEARING] And at your service, from then on in.

GITTEL [GLUMLY] For how long?

JERRY Hey?

GITTEL I said for how long.

JERRY Can't hear you.

(He turns off the water and comes in, drying his face with a towel.)

Hm?

GITTEL I said I love you.

*(*JERRY *stands absolutely still for a long moment. Then* GITTEL *lowers her eyes.)*

Hell, I don't have to say it, do I? You know it.

JERRY [GENTLY] Yes.

GITTEL I'll try not to say it too often. Twice a week.

JERRY You can't say it too often, it's part of my new muscle.

GITTEL Maybe getting sick was the biggest favor I ever did you, huh?

JERRY I think we can manage without. The big favor is to get back on your feet, Gittel.

(GITTEL'S *eyes are down.* JERRY *glances at his watch, bends to kiss her cheek, and crosses to the bureau.*)

GITTEL [LOW] What's the percentage?

(JERRY *opening a drawer frowns. He then takes out a laundered shirt, removes the cardboard, and slips into the shirt.*)

JERRY The percentage is one hundred.

GITTEL I don't mean to get better, I mean—

JERRY I know what you mean. When I said I'd like to look out for you what do you think *I* meant, a thirty-day option?

(*Buttoning his shirt he goes back into the kitchen, where he turns the potatoes off and puts a plate in the oven to warm.*)

You ready for lunch?

GITTEL You eat already?

JERRY I'll take a sandwich into the office. You wouldn't care to spring to your feet and run around the plate three times, work up an appetite?

(*He waits on her in the doorway; she does not meet his eyes.*)

GITTEL I got an appetite.

JERRY A hm.

(Presently he turns back into the kitchen, where he prepares a tray—tumbler of milk, paper napkin, silverware, and the meal on a plate.)

GITTEL You ought to have more than a sandwich, Jerry, you get sick too we'll really be up the goddam creek. Get a malted, too, huh? And tell him make it a guggle-muggle while he's at it.

JERRY A what?

GITTEL It's with a beat-up egg. I mean two whole days of exam, you got to keep your strength up for those cruds.

*(*JERRY *brings in the tray, and places it on her lap in bed.)*

JERRY The condemned man ate a hearty guggle-muggle and lived another thirty-four years. I don't intend to get sick, infant, even to get you up.

(He collects papers and books on the table, slipping them into his brief case, and pauses over the legal document he has dropped there; he takes it up, and with his back to GITTEL *reads it again, grimly.)*

GITTEL Jerry.

JERRY Yes.

GITTEL [PAINFULLY] I'm not just taking advantage, you know, I'm—I mean since you been living here I'm—Nobody ever took care of me so good, it sort of weakens your will power, you know?

(JERRY *looks over his shoulder at her, then back at the document; he is deliberating between them.*)

JERRY Strengthens mine.

GITTEL I mean I'm kind of in the habit of—seeing your neckties around, now. I'll miss them.

(*A silence,* JERRY *weighing the document and something else, much heavier, in himself.*)

JERRY [THEN] Why do you think I'm taking this Bar exam, you boob, to lift legal dumbbells? I intend to live here, work here, be used. Lot of my life I've been cold from being unused.

GITTEL I'm scared of afterwards, Jerry.

JERRY What's afterwards?

GITTEL I get up out of here, all the goddam neckties go back to your place. I'm scared to—live alone, again. Now.

(JERRY *stands for a long moment with the document. Then abruptly and decisively he wads it into his briefcase, sits, thrusts books and papers away to clear space, and writes.*)

JERRY Eat your lunch.

(GITTEL *obeys, for a mouthful or two, but watches him perplexedly.*)

GITTEL What are you writing?

JERRY A promissory note. I promise you, conversation at meals.

(*When he is finished he folds the paper; standing, he takes up the gift box.*)

And other items, less elevating.

(He lifts out a Chinese bed jacket of brocaded silk. GITTEL *drops her fork.)*

GITTEL Hey! That's *beautiful,* what is it?

JERRY Something to remember me by, till six o'clock.

GITTEL A bed jacket! Ye gods, I'll never get up.

(She wiggles her fingers for it, but JERRY *holds up the folded paper.)*

JERRY This is a letter to my landlord.

(He slips it into the pocket of the bed jacket.)

For *you* to mail. By hand.

GITTEL Huh?

JERRY At the corner. As soon as you're on your feet to make it down there.

GITTEL Why, what's it say?

(Her eyes widen.)

Get a new tenant! Huh?

JERRY See for yourself.

GITTEL You'll move the neckties in for keeps?

JERRY See for yourself.

(From across the room he holds the bed jacket ready for her, the letter poking out prominently.)

GITTEL [REPROACHFULLY] Jerry.

JERRY Come and get it.

GITTEL [REPROACHFULLY] Jerry, I got to be on my feet to get you?

JERRY Maybe. Better find out, hm?

(GITTEL *shakes her head.*)

Is it so out of the question that I want to keep the goddam neckties here? Come on.

(GITTEL *just gazes at him, her eyes moist.*)

Come. Come and get it.

(GITTEL *puts the tray aside, moves her legs to the edge, and sits still.*)

Come on, honey.

(GITTEL *stands, unsteady for a moment, then moves toward him, afraid of her belly, afraid of her legs, the progress of someone who hasn't walked in a month; but she gets to him and the letter, unfolds it, and reads.*)

GITTEL You're giving up your flat.

JERRY Save rent.

GITTEL [A PAUSE] You're really ruining me, Jerry!

(*She keeps her face averted, on the verge of tears.*)

I didn't use to be a—bitch of a—lousy blackmailer.

(*Another pause*)

And I'm not going to be either! Enough is enough!

(*And with sudden resolution she tears the letter into pieces.*)

JERRY [EQUABLY] That's how you waste forest resources? Now I'll have to write another.

GITTEL Not unless you want to!

JERRY I want to.

(His arms wrap her in the bed jacket, and hold her. He kisses her, studies her eyes; she searches his. Then he glances at his watch, pats her cheek, and reaches for his brief case.)

Don't overdo a good thing. Lie down soon. Chew your lunch before swallowing. Take your medicine. Don't tackle the stairs alone. Button up your overcoat, you belong to me.

(He is on his way to the door, when her small voice stops him.)

GITTEL Jerry. I do. You know I do, now?

JERRY Yes. I know that, infant.

GITTEL I love you.

(JERRY stands inarticulate, until she releases him:)

That's twice, there, I used up the whole week!

JERRY [LIGHTLY] I may need to hear it again before that Bar exam. For muscle.

GITTEL You'll pass.

JERRY Hell, I'll blow all the answers out of my brilliant nose.

(He blows her a kiss and is out the door, gone, leaving her on her feet in the room, shaking her head after him, in her Chinese silk, like a rainbow, half radiance, half tears. She fingers his coat, sits, and brings it to her face; she is much troubled.)

Scene 2

JERRY'S ROOM. IT IS MAY, ALMOST SUMMER NOW, A HOT MUGGY DUSK, AND EIGHT MONTHS SINCE THIS AFFAIR BEGAN. ONCE AGAIN THE WINDOWS OF BOTH ROOMS ARE OPEN—JERRY'S FROM THE TOP—AND THE SOUNDS OF TRAFFIC FLOAT IN.

In GITTEL'S *room the only change is that the table is cleared of all* JERRY'S *exam preparations, the night table is cleared of medicines, the bed is made.*

JERRY'S *flat however is a shambles. Packing is in progress, nothing is in its place, cartons stand here and there. In the kitchen* JERRY *in his shirt sleeves is slowly wrapping dishware in newspaper; in the living room* GITTEL*—barefoot and back to normal, but with a stratum of gloom underneath—is folding linens into a carton. This separate activity goes on for an interval of silence, until* JERRY *calls in; his voice is rather dispirited, and so is hers.*

JERRY What about these pots, honey? You want them packed separate?

GITTEL Separate from what?

JERRY Dishes.

GITTEL Guess so. I mean, sure.

(They go back to packing in silence. Both are sweaty with the prosaic drudgery of packing, and depressed, but neither is admitting this; there is an atmosphere of something being avoided. Then GITTEL *stands on a chair to take down the clothes-closet curtain, and in the process jogs one support of the rod with its remaining clothes; it falls.* GITTEL *grabs it.)*

Help!

*(*JERRY *drops what he is doing, and comes at once, on the run.)*

JERRY What's wrong?

GITTEL This cruddy pole. S'all.

JERRY [RELIEVED] Oh. I thought you—

(He stops himself, takes the rod and clothes off her hands, and lays them on the couch.)

Never did get around to fixing that thing permanently. Guess I never believed it was permanent, all it takes is two screws and a—

(He becomes aware of her eyes moody on him.)

Hm?

GITTEL Nothing.

(They gaze at each other a moment, something unsaid between them. Then JERRY *grips her at the waist, and lifts her down.)*

JERRY You stay on the ground, squirrel.

GITTEL [IRKED] Why?

JERRY Because I've climbed Long's Peak four times. I'm used to these rare altitudes.

(He climbs the chair, and begins to unhook the curtain.)

GITTEL What'd you think, I was doing a nose dive? No such luck.

JERRY [ANOTHER GAZE] What kind of cheery remark is that?

GITTEL I mean *bad* luck.

JERRY Oh. I thought you meant good bad luck.

GITTEL What's Long's Peak?

JERRY Mountain. Front Range, Colorado. Fourteen thousand feet, up on all fours, down on all fives.

GITTEL [A PAUSE] I been up the Empire State nineteen times, so what?

*(*JERRY *smiles, shakes his head, and turns to hand her the curtain.)*

JERRY Here.

(But GITTEL *is on her way out to the kitchen, in a mood.* JERRY *stares, tosses the curtain onto the couch mattress, bare in its ticking, and considers the window drapes.)*

You want this other one down?

GITTEL [OUT OF SIGHT] What other one?

JERRY Window curtain.

GITTEL D'*you* want it down?

JERRY [PUZZLED] Yes, I want it down.

GITTEL So take it down!

JERRY [FROWNING] What's eating you?

GITTEL A banana!

JERRY What?

GITTEL A banana.

(*She comes in again, eating a banana.*)

Want a bite?

JERRY I said, what's eating *you.*

(*He moves the chair to the window, gets up again, and works on the burlap drapes.*)

GITTEL Oh, *me.* What's eating you.

JERRY I asked you first.

GITTEL I mean what's eating me is figuring out what's eating you.

JERRY I see. Well, what's eating me is figuring out what's eating you. Which just about exhausts that investigation. Be altogether fruitless except for the banana. Want these brackets too?

(GITTEL *not replying bites at the banana, and* JERRY *looks from the brackets down to her.*)

Hm?

GITTEL *I* don't want a goddam thing. D'*you* want them?

JERRY [A PAUSE] Correction. Do *we* want them?

GITTEL We sure do. Cost good money, can always use them.

JERRY That's right, ten cents a pair. I'll get a screwdriver.

(*He comes down, to head for the kitchen.*)

GITTEL So then don't!

JERRY I mean what do we need *all* this junk for? We have your curtains there, we're not going to—

GITTEL What junk?

(*She is handling the drapes, pinches up a piece.*)

That's good stuff, forty-seven cents a yard reduced, I could make eleven different things out of it.

JERRY Name ten.

GITTEL Anything. Bedspread, cushions, pocketbook, I was even thinking I'd make you some neckties.

JERRY [VERY DUBIOUS] Well.

GITTEL You don't want?

JERRY I just don't see myself appearing in court in a red burlap necktie.

(*He goes into the kitchen.* GITTEL *takes up the banana again for a last bite, slings the peel straight across the room out the open window, and sits gloomily on the couch.* JERRY *returning with the screwdriver studies her as he passes.*)

Maybe we ought to knock off for tonight, infant. You look tired.

GITTEL [TESTILY] I'm not tired!

JERRY Then why so down?

GITTEL *Who's* down? I'm in sixth heaven!

(JERRY *stops to eye her before mounting the chair.*)

Just don't rush to the rescue. You're killing me with kindness.

(JERRY *after a moment plunges the screwdriver by the handle straight into the chair, and lets it stand;* GITTEL'S *eyes widen. But* JERRY *shows no further vehemence, and when he speaks it is calmly enough.*)

JERRY That's in exchange for all the little needles.

GITTEL [SULLEN] I'm sorry.

JERRY We're supposed to be joyfully packing to be together. Why act as though—

GITTEL Nobody around here's *enjoying* this. Every frigging towel I put in that box I feel worse.

JERRY [DRYLY] It's a chore, who likes to break up a happy home?

(*He fishes in his shirt pocket for cigarettes.*)

Though in a peculiar way it has been. I won't forget *this* first-aid station in a hurry.

GITTEL There's always the next one.

JERRY What next one?

GITTEL The one we're fixing up for me.

(JERRY *looks at her, lights the cigarette, and to avoid the topic mounts the chair again with the screwdriver.* GITTEL *takes a fresh breath and dives in, very brightly.*)

Look, Jerry, whyn't we just, sort of, get married and get the goddam thing over with, huh?

(JERRY *half-turns, to gaze at her over his shoulder.*)

JERRY Bigamy? Big of you, I mean, I have one wife now.

GITTEL I mean *after* the divorce. I'm not going to be just a ball and chain, now you passed that Bar exam you know the first thing I'm going to do? Take up shorthand!

JERRY Shorthand is the one thing this romance has lacked from the beginning.

GITTEL So when you open your law office, there I am! A goddam secretary, you're really going to save dough on me. And soon as I make enough out of that loft I'm going to fix up the flat for us, real nice.

JERRY It's real nice.

GITTEL Stinks.

JERRY What stinks about it?

GITTEL It's a dump, you think I don't know that? My God, how can you entertain somebody a cockroach committee comes out of the sink to see who's here? Hasn't been an exterminator in there since Babe Ruth.

JERRY Who are we exterminating?

GITTEL Huh?

JERRY I meant to say entertaining.

GITTEL Well, anybody you need to. Customers! Partners, the Taubmans, maybe *criminals*, you don't know who yet, but you can't have a dump for them. Can you?

JERRY [A PAUSE] No. I couldn't think of representing some dope addict who'd just murdered his mother and have him see a cockroach. Here's the brackets.

(*But* GITTEL *is folding the drapes to put in the carton, and he steps down with them.*)

GITTEL Who knows, maybe later on we'll move to a real

apartment house even. You know one thing I always wanted to live in a house with?

JERRY Me?

GITTEL An elevator! With an elevator you can invite anybody.

*(*JERRY *drops the brackets in her purse, next to her little radio. The radio stops him, he contemplates it, rubs it with his thumb, and then finds* GITTEL's *eye on him.)*

JERRY [SMILES] Remembering the day you left this at the door. We kept each other company many a wee hour, I hate to see it end up all alone in some closet.

GITTEL Nah, we'll use it.

JERRY [MILDLY] If you have in mind plastic neckties, they're also out. I have room for it in with the pots.

(He takes the radio out into the kitchen. GITTEL *on her knees begins on another carton, loading in books, papers, a miscellany.)*

GITTEL [CALLING OUT] What about this stuff, Jerry, bills? Gas, phone—

JERRY [OUT OF SIGHT] Leave them out where I'll see them, I don't think I paid those yet.

GITTEL [DISCARDING THEM] What do you want to pay them, all they can do is shut it off if you do or you don't. Letters—

(She unfolds one, on feminine blue stationery.)

"Jerry dearest, I—" Whoops.

(She shuts it in a hurry, not reading it, but as she puts it away she comes to a legal document

in blue backing that tickles her memory: the last time she saw it was in her room, in JERRY'S *hands. She reads, frowning, her lips moving at first soundlessly, then becoming audible.*)

"—although the plaintiff has conducted herself as a true and faithful wife to the defendant, the said defendant has been guilty. Of acts of cruelty toward the plaintiff, destroying the—"

(*Now* JERRY *is standing in the doorway, a cup in his hand.*)

"—peace of mind of the plaintiff and the objects of —matrimony. It is hereby ordered, adjudged—"

(JERRY *completes it from memory.*)

JERRY [SLOWLY] —and decreed by the Court that the bonds of matrimony heretofore existing are severed and held for naught. And that the said plaintiff is granted an absolute divorce from the defendant. Unquote.

(*A silence*)

GITTEL So why didn't you tell me, Jerry.

JERRY [A PAUSE] I had to live with it. A while longer. Digest it. Let it grow out with my fingernails, till I was—rid of it.

(*Another pause*)

GITTEL You didn't want me to know.

JERRY Not till I was—on top of it. Do you know what the sense of never is? Never again, not even once? Never is a deep hole, it takes time to—close over.

GITTEL Then what'll you do?

JERRY Then?

GITTEL Yeah. Then.

JERRY [A PAUSE, GENTLY] I think I'll do one thing at a time.

GITTEL What?

JERRY Pack this cup.

(He comes to the carton with it, kneeling near her.)

GITTEL You sonofabitch.

*(*JERRY *wheels on his knee to confront her.)*

You tell her about *me?* That you moved in?

JERRY [WHITELY] Yes.

GITTEL Because I had a hemorrhage?

JERRY I'm *not* a sonofabitch—

GITTEL *Did you tell her I had a hemorrhage?*

JERRY Yes.

GITTEL And you didn't tell me about this?

(She slings the decree straight into his face. JERRY *squats, rigid.* GITTEL *then scrambles up and makes for her shoes.* JERRY *rising slams the cup into the carton of crockery.)*

Smash them all, who needs them?

JERRY What are you off on this time?

GITTEL I'm getting out of here, you—you goddam—

(But the grief breaks through, and she wails to him out of loss:)

Jerry, *why* didn't you *tell* me?

JERRY I couldn't.

(GITTEL *gazing at him takes this in; then she finishes putting her shoes on, and makes a beeline for her bag.*)

GITTEL Yeah. You only tell her about me. My God, even when you *divorce* her it's a secret you have with her! One of these days you'll marry me, she'll know it and I won't!

(*But when she turns to the doorway,* JERRY *is planted in it, blocking her.*)

JERRY You're not leaving.

GITTEL Jerry, look out!

JERRY Sit down.

GITTEL You look out or I'll let you have it, Jerry!

JERRY Go ahead, street brawler.

(GITTEL *slaps him across the face, he is unmoving; she slaps him again backhand, he is like a statue; she then wheels looking for a weapon, comes up from the carton with the broken cup, and charges his face, but hesitates.* JERRY *stands moveless, waiting.*)

Do. I'll beat your behind off.

(GITTEL *flinging the cup past him throws herself averted on the couch, tearful with rage.*)

GITTEL Sonofabitch, all my life I never yet could beat up one goddam man, it's just *no* fair!

JERRY Why do you think I told her about the hemorrhage?

GITTEL To prove something to her on *me,* now.

JERRY Like what?

GITTEL How you're so wonderful, looking after me, you don't need her help.

JERRY I told her because she asked *my* help. She wants me home.

(GITTEL *rolls over, to stare at him.*)

GITTEL She does.

JERRY When at last she really needs me, and I'm enough my own man to help, I had to say no. And why.

GITTEL [A DEEP BREATH] Okay, Jerry. You said make a claim, right?

JERRY Yes.

GITTEL So I'm going to make it.

JERRY All right.

GITTEL I want you here. I want *all* of you here. I don't want half a hunk of you, I want—I mean it's—

(*With difficulty*)

It's leap year, Jerry, tell the truth. *Would* you—ever say—I love you? Once.

JERRY [PAINED] It's a lifetime promise, infant, I've only said it once.

(*But the moment he turns again to the kitchen, her voice rises after him:*)

GITTEL Jerry, Jerry, give me a break, will you? Don't kid me along. Is that a friend?

(*This word nails him, he turns back with his eyes moist.*)

I'll tell you straight, you move in I just—won't give up on you marrying me. You—you let me have it straight, too.

(*He stands, gazing at her.*)

Jerry, you my friend?

JERRY [FINALLY] I'm your friend. Here it is, straight. You say love, I think you mean *in* love. I mean so much more by that word now—

GITTEL I mean wanting. Somebody. So bad—

JERRY Not wanting. Love is having, having had, having had so—deeply, daily, year in and out, that a man and woman exchange—guts, minds, memories, exchange—eyes. Love is seeing through the other's eyes. So because she likes bridges I never see a bridge here without grief, that her eyes are not looking. A hundred things like that. Not simply friend, some ways my mortal enemy, but *wife*, and ingrown.

(*He looks down at the decree.*)

What *could* I tell you about this—piece of paper, that the bonds of matrimony are *not* severed? Why would I—love my right hand, if I lost it? That's what love is. To me, now.

(GITTEL *keeps her eyes on him for a long moment, then she closes them.*)

GITTEL You ever tell her that?

JERRY No. I should have told her years ago, I didn't know it then.

(GITTEL *rolls up; she climbs the chair at the window and hangs gazing out, to find her way through this.*)

GITTEL You'll never marry me, Jerry.

JERRY I can't, infant.

GITTEL So what kind of competition can I give her, have a

hemorrhage twice a year? Trap you that way, be *more* of a cripple, one month to another? Get half of you by being a wreck on your hands, will that keep you around?

JERRY As long as you need me, I'll be around.

(GITTEL *turns on the chair, staring at him, as it dawns on her.*)

GITTEL And you'll move in. Even now.

JERRY What's in me to give, without shortchanging, I'll give—

GITTEL My God, *I'm* in a goddam trap!

(*A pause; then* JERRY *nods.*)

You're one, all right, I could—lose a leg or something in you.

JERRY Yes, you could lose—a lot of time. You're a growing girl, and of the two things I really want, one is to see you grow. And bear your fruit.

GITTEL And the other is—

JERRY Tess.

GITTEL Jerry, Jerry, Jerry.

(*She regards him, her eyes blinking; this is hard to say.*)

I don't *want* the short end. I want somebody'll—say to me what you just said about her.

(*She gets down, retrieving her bag, and stands not looking at him.*)

What do you say we—give each other the gate, huh, Jerry?

(She moves to pass him in the doorway; but he stops her, to take her face between his palms, and search her eyes.)

JERRY For whose sake?

GITTEL Jerry, I haven't taken one happy breath since that hemorrhage. I want to get out of here and *breathe.*

(After a moment JERRY *lets her go. She brushes quickly past him, through the kitchen and out of the flat. He turns in the doorway, looking after her, with his hands up on the jambs, unmoving as the lights dim.)*

Scene 3 BOTH ROOMS. IT IS A FEW DAYS LATER, A GRAY AFTERNOON.

JERRY'S *room is cleaned out, altogether bare except for his suitcase and portable typewriter standing there, and the phone on the floor near them.* JERRY *is not in sight, though we may hear him in the kitchen.*

GITTEL *is in her room, taking the dance photos of herself down from the wall. She is engaged in this without feeling, almost without awareness; it is something to do while she waits. What she is waiting for is the phone, as we see from her eyes. She takes the photos to her night table and drops them in a drawer, then walks nervously round and round her room, eyeing her alarm clock, eyeing her phone.*

Meanwhile a match has been lighted in JERRY'S *dark kitchen,* JERRY *making a last survey of it. When he comes in, he is in street clothes and hat; he is shaking the match out, his other arm cradles a few last toilet articles, shaving cream, brush, razor. He kneels at the typewriter case, and fits these articles carefully in. Then he consults his wrist watch. He stands over the phone a heavy moment, picks it up, and dials.*

The phone in GITTEL*'s room rings, and she flies to sit on her bed.*

GITTEL Yeah, hello?

JERRY [A PAUSE] Honey, I'm—all packed here, I—

GITTEL [SOFTLY] Hiya, Jerry.

JERRY [A PAUSE] Some cartons of—odds and ends in the kitchen here, the key will be with the janitor. If you want anything.

GITTEL I won't want anything.

JERRY If you do.

(*A pause*)

Look, if you do, I mean anything—important, Gittel, I'm at the Commodore Hotel in Lincoln, I don't have the number, long-distance will give it to you. Lincoln, Nebraska. *Not* Nevada.

GITTEL Not Nevada.

JERRY And not Omaha, I'm not walking back into that mistake, ever again. As soon as I get an office and a phone I'll send you the number. Now if you—if you need anything in a hurry, I mean instantly, will you call Frank Taubman? You won't have to explain anything, it's taken care of, just call him.

GITTEL [A PAUSE] Yeah.

JERRY No. Promise.

GITTEL I promise.

(*A pause*)

Jerry, I'm all right now. You just—you just get what you want out there, huh?

JERRY I'll try. It's back to the wars. My terms are steep, I won't work for Lucian, I won't live in Omaha, and all we'll have is what I earn. I'm beginning very—modestly, a desk and a phone and a pencil. And what's in my head.

GITTEL It's a lot.

JERRY But I won't shortchange her. It has to be a new deal, on both sides.

GITTEL I'm rooting for you, Jerry.

JERRY No backsliding. By you either, Gittel, don't you give up either, hm?

GITTEL Oh, I don't! I bounce up, like a—jack in the box, you know?

JERRY I'm rooting for you, too. It's a big city and you're the salt of the earth, just don't waste it, he's around some corner. You'll find him.

GITTEL I'm looking. I got a better opinion of myself now, I'm going to propose more often. I'll send you a birthday card now and then, huh?

JERRY Now and then.

GITTEL Twice a week!

(JERRY *pinches his eyes, he is shaky.*)

JERRY Gittel. What am I doing, I—moments here I think I—

GITTEL You're doing right, Jerry. I mean *I* don't want any handouts either, you know? That's no favor.

JERRY If I know anything I know that.

GITTEL And I'm not going to be just giving them out, from now on. I want somebody'll take care of me who's all mine. You taught me that. And nobody like Sam or Jake, between them they couldn't take care of a chiclet. I mean, things look a lot different to me, Jerry, you did me a world of good.

JERRY Did I really? Golly, if I could think each of us—helped somehow, helped a bit—

GITTEL You been a great help, Jerry, it's the first affair I—come out with more than I went in. I mean, wherever this guy is, he'll owe you!

JERRY [A PAUSE, HUMBLY] Thank you for that. And she'll owe you more than she'll know. After—

(*He tries to recall it.*)

After the verb to love, to help is—

GITTEL [A PAUSE] What, Jerry?

JERRY —the sweetest in the tongue. Somebody said it. Well.

(*He looks at his watch.*)

Well. So long, infant.

(GITTEL *tries to say it, but her eyes are full, her heart is in her mouth, and she struggles to keep it from overflowing there; she cannot.*)

GITTEL *I love you, Jerry!*

(JERRY *is rigid; it takes her a moment to go on.*)

Long as you *live* I want you to remember the last thing you heard out of me was I love you!

JERRY [LONG PAUSE] I love you too, Gittel.

(He hangs up, and for a moment there is no movement.

Then JERRY *puts the phone down, and lights himself a cigarette; his first drag tells us how much he needs it. After another, he kneels again, shuts the typewriter case, stands with it and the suitcase in either hand, and gives the room a final check.*

GITTEL *meanwhile has not hung up; she clicks down, then rapidly dials again. But the minute it rings once, she claps the phone down.*

JERRY *is on his way out with typewriter and suitcase when the single ring comes. He stops, not putting either down, just staring at the phone for a long minute.* GITTEL *sits, head high, eyes closed. Neither moves.*

Then GITTEL *takes her hand off the phone. And* JERRY *turns, and walks out of his flat.)*

A NOTE ON THE AUTHOR

WILLIAM GIBSON was born in the Highbridge section of the Bronx, New York, in 1914. He was educated in the New York City public schools, at Townsend Harris Hall, and at the City College of New York. His previously published work includes a short verse play, *I Lay in Zion* (1947); a volume of poems, *Winter Crook* (1948); a novel, *The Cobweb* (1954); a play for television, *The Miracle Worker* (1957); and numerous poems and short stories in such periodicals as *The American Scholar, Poetry, The New Yorker, Harper's Bazaar,* and *Partisan Review.* With his wife and two sons, William Gibson makes his home in Stockbridge, Massachusetts.

A NOTE ON THE TYPE

This book is set in ELECTRA, *a Linotype face designed by* W. A. DWIGGINS (1880-1956), *who was responsible for so much that is good in contemporary book design. Although much of his early work was in advertising and he was the author of the standard volume* Layout in Advertising, *Mr. Dwiggins later devoted his prolific talents to book typography and type design, and worked with great distinction in both fields. In addition to his designs for Electra, he created the Metro, Caledonia, and Eldorado series of type faces, as well as a number of experimental cuttings that have never been issued commercially.*

Electra cannot be classified as either modern or old-style. It is not based on any historical model, nor does it echo a particular period or style. It avoids the extreme contrast between thick and thin elements which marks most modern faces, and attempts to give a feeling of fluidity, power, and speed.

This book was composed, printed, and bound by H. WOLFF, *New York. The paper was manufactured by* S. D. WARREN CO., *Boston. Design by* GUY FLEMING.